United States
Department of
Agriculture

Forest Service

Northern
Research Station

Resource Bulletin
NRS-60

# South Dakota's Forests, 2005: Statistics, Methods, and Quality Assurance

Patrick D. Miles, Ronald J. Piva, Charles J. Barnett

## Abstract

The first full annual inventory of South Dakota's forests was completed in 2005 after 8,302 plots were selected and 325 forested plots were visited and measured. This report includes detailed information on forest inventory methods and data quality estimates. Important resource statistics are included in the tables. A detailed analysis of the South Dakota inventory is presented in Resource Bulletin NRS-35 (www.nrs.fs.fed.us/pubs/rb/rb_nrs35.pdf).

## The Authors

PATRICK D. MILES is a research forester with the Forest Inventory and Analysis program, Northern Research Station, St. Paul, MN.

RONALD J. PIVA is a forester with the Forest Inventory and Analysis program, Northern Research Station, St. Paul, MN.

CHARLES J. BARNETT is a forester with the Forest Inventory and Analysis program, Northern Research Station, Newtown Square, PA.

# CONTENTS

# FOREST INVENTORY METHODS
## Strategic Model

The Forest Inventory and Analysis (FIA) program of the Northern Research Station (NRS) is part of the national enhanced FIA program that focuses on six strategic objectives (McRoberts 2005):
- A standard set of variables with nationally consistent meanings and measurements
- Field inventories of all forested lands
- Nationally consistent estimation
- Adherence to national precision standards
- Consistent reporting and data distribution
- Credibility with users and stakeholders

To ensure that these objectives are achieved, 10 strategic approaches have been prescribed:
- A national set of prescribed core variables with a national field manual that describes measurement procedures and protocols for each variable
- A national plot configuration
- A nationally consistent sampling design
- Estimation using standardized formulae for sample-based estimators
- A national database of FIA data with core standards and user-friendly public access
- A national information management system
- A nationally consistent set of tables with estimates of prescribed core variables
- Publication of statewide tables with estimates of prescribed core variables at 5-year intervals.
- Documentation of the technical aspects of the FIA program including procedures, protocols, and techniques
- Peer review and publication of the technical documentation for general access

The result of this approach is an inventory program with new features and a nationally consistent plot configuration, a nationally consistent sampling design for all lands, annual measurement of a proportion of plots in each state, nationally consistent estimation techniques and algorithms, and integration of the ground-sampling components of the FIA inventory and detection monitoring by the USDA Forest Service's Forest Health Monitoring (FHM) program.

## Plot Configuration

The national FIA plot design (Fig. 1) consists of four circular 24-ft-radius subplots (1/24th acre) configured as a central subplot and three peripheral subplots. Centers of the peripheral subplots are 120 ft from the central subplot and at azimuths of 360°, 120°, and 240° from the center of the central subplot. Trees with a diameter at breast height (d.b.h.) of 5 inches or greater are measured on these subplots. Each subplot contains a circular 6.8-ft-radius microplot (1/300th acre) with the center located 12 ft east of the subplot center on which each tree at least 1 inch but less than 5 inches d.b.h. is measured. Forest conditions having area of 1 acre or greater that occur on any of the four subplots are mapped on the subplot and recorded. Factors that differentiate forest conditions include forest type, stand-size class, stand origin, land use, ownership, and density. Macroplots are not used by NRS-FIA. They have a radius of 58.9 ft and are used for sampling intensification or for sampling relatively rare events. The 1/4-acre macroplot currently is used by the Rocky Mountain and Pacific Northwest Stations' FIA programs to sample large trees.

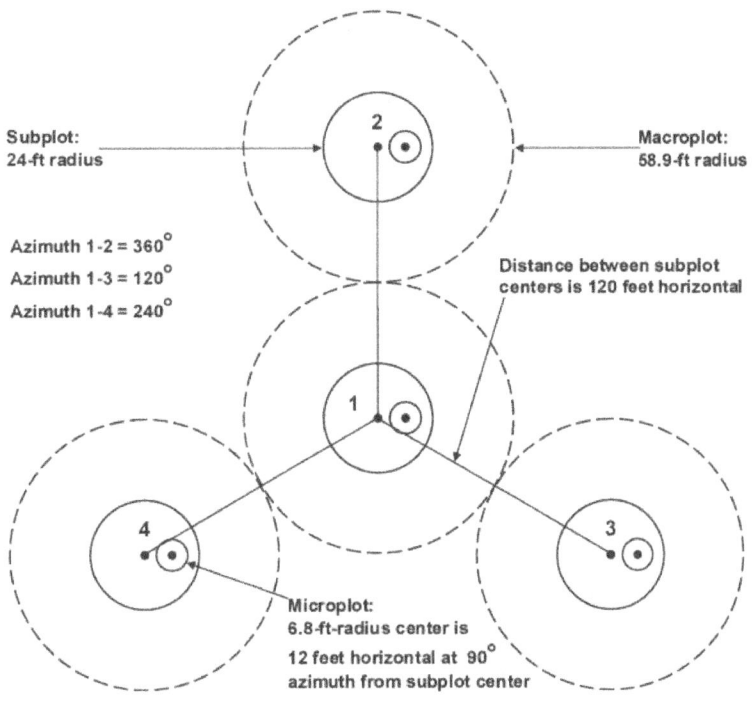

Figure 1. National FIA plot design (adapted from Bechtold and Patterson 2005).

## Sample Design

On the basis of historical sampling errors, a sampling intensity of about one plot per 6,000 acres is necessary to satisfy national FIA precision guidelines. Therefore, FIA divided the area of the United States into nonoverlapping, 5,937-acre hexagons and established a plot in each hexagon as follows: 1) if an existing FHM plot was located in a hexagon, it was selected; 2) if there was no FHM plot in the hexagon, the existing FIA plot from the previous periodic inventory nearest the hexagon center was selected; and 3) if neither an FHM nor an FIA plot was located in the hexagon, a new FIA plot was established at a random location in the hexagon (Brand et al. 2000, McRoberts 1999). This array of field plots is designated the Federal base sample and is considered an equal probability sample; measurement of the Federal base sample is funded by the Federal Government.

The Federal base sample is divided into five interpenetrating, nonoverlapping panels or subsamples, each of which provides complete, systematic coverage of a state. Each year, plots in a single panel are measured; panels are selected on a 5-year, rotating basis (McRoberts 1999). For estimation purposes, the measurement of each panel of plots is considered an independent, equal probability sample of all lands in a state.

## Three-Phase Inventory

FIA conducts inventories in three phases. Remotely sensed data are used in Phase 1 to classify the area in the population of interest, for latter use in the post-stratification process, to increase the precision of estimates. In Phase 2, field crews visit the physical locations of permanent field plots to measure traditional inventory variables such as tree species, diameter, and height. In Phase 3, field crews visit a subset of Phase 2 plots to obtain measurements for an additional suite of variables associated with forest and ecosystem health. The three phases of the enhanced FIA program as implemented in this inventory are discussed in detail in the sections that follow.

## Phase 1

Aerial photographs, digital orthoquads (DOQs: digitally scanned aerial photograph), and satellite imagery are used for initial plot measurement via remotely sensed data and stratification. Phase 1 plot measurement consists of observations of conditions at the plot locations using aerial photographs or DOQs. Analysts determine a digitized geographic location for each field plot and a human interpreter assigns to the plot a land cover/use with primary focus on identifying forest land.[1] All plot locations that could contain forest land are selected for further measurement via field-crew visits in Phase 2.

The combination of natural variability among plots and budgetary constraints prohibits measurement of a sufficient number of plots to satisfy national precision standards for most inventory variables unless the estimation process is enhanced using ancillary data. Thus, the land area is stratified using remotely sensed and other map-based data.

A stratification scheme based on satellite imagery as proposed by Hansen and Wendt (2000) is applied to the National Land Cover Data (NLCD) as suggested by McRoberts et al. (2002). The NLCD is a digital land-cover map of the conterminous United States in which 30- by 30-m pixels are assigned to 21 land-cover classes. This classification was produced by the U.S. Geological Survey and was based on nominal 1992 Landsat 5 Thematic Mapper (TM) satellite imagery and data (Vogelmann et al. 2001). Four strata are created using a three-step process: 1) aggregate NLCD classes with trees into a forest stratum with the remaining classes into a nonforest stratum; 2) reclassify isolated groups of three or fewer pixels into their surrounding forest or nonforest class to comply with the FIA criterion that forest land must be at least 1 acre; and 3) create two additional classes (forest edge and nonforest edge) that includes all pixels within two pixels of the forest/nonforest boundary.

In addition to classifying every pixel into one of the four strata, for 10 of the 11 estimation units every pixel was assigned to an ownership strata based on the Protected Areas Database (PAD) described by DellaSala et al. (2001). The PAD was not used to assign ownership for the Minnesota-Big Sioux-Cote estimation unit (the 18 eastern most counties of South Dakota). Almost all of the land in the Minnesota-Big Sioux-Cote estimation unit is in private ownership and 91 percent of the forest land in this estimation unit is in private ownership.

Stratified estimation requires that two tasks be accomplished. First, each plot must be assigned to a single stratum. Next, the proportion of each detailed stratum must be calculated (TM land-cover classification and ownership group delineation). The first task is accomplished by assigning each plot to the stratum assigned for the pixel containing the center of the center subplot. The second task is

---

[1] Lands satisfying FIA's definition of forest land include commercial timberland, some pastured land with trees, forest plantations, unproductive forested land, and reserved, noncommercial forested land. Forest land requires minimum stocking levels, a 1 acre minimum area, and a minimum bole to bole width of 120 ft with continuous canopy. Forest land excludes wooded strips and windbreaks less than 120 ft wide and idle farmland or other previously nonforest land that currently is below minimum stocking levels.

accomplished by calculating the proportion of pixels in each stratum. The population estimate for a variable is calculated as the sum across all strata of the product of each stratum's observed proportion (from Phase 1) and the variable's estimated mean per unit area for the stratum (from Phase 2). Details of the stratum assignments used in South Dakota are discussed in the estimation section of this report.

## Phase 2

In Phase 2, field crews record a variety of data for plot locations determined in Phase 1 to include accessible forest land. Before visiting plot locations, field crews consult county land records to determine the ownership of plots and then seek permission from private landowners to measure plots on their lands. At the plot, field crews determine the location of the geographic center of the center subplot using GPS receivers. They record condition-level observations that include land cover, forest type, stand origin, stand age, stand-size class, site-productivity class, history of forest disturbance, and land use for every condition (major land use or forest stand at least 1 acre in size) that occurs on the plot. They also record information on condition boundaries on plots with multiple conditions. For each tree, field crews record a variety of observations and measurements, including condition, species, live/dead status, lean, diameter, height, crown ratio (percentage of tree height represented by crown), crown class (dominant, codominant, suppressed), damage, and decay status. Office staff use statistical models based on field-crew measurements to calculate values for additional variables, including individual-tree volume, per-unit-area estimates of number of trees, volume, and biomass by plot, condition, species group, and live/dead status. Additional information on data collection procedures used in Phase 2 is available at http://www.nrs.fs.fed.us/fia/data-collection/.

## Phase 3

The third phase of the enhanced FIA program focuses on forest health. Phase 3 is administered by the FIA program with consultation from other Forest Service programs, other Federal agencies, state natural resource agencies, universities, and the FHM program. The FHM program consists of four interrelated and complementary activities: detection, evaluation, intensive site-ecosystem monitoring, and research on monitoring techniques. Detection monitoring consists of systematic aerial and ground surveys designed to collect baseline information on the current condition of forest ecosystems and to detect changes from those baselines over time. Evaluation studies examine the extent, severity, and probable causes of changes in forest health identified through the detection monitoring surveys. Intensive site-ecosystem monitoring examines regionally specific ecological processes at a network of sites in representative forested ecosystems. Research on monitoring techniques focuses on developing and refining indicator measurements to improve the efficiency and reliability of data collection and analysis at all levels of the program.

The ground-survey portion of the detection-monitoring program was integrated into the FIA program as Phase 3 in 1999. The Phase 3 sample consists of a 1:16 subset of the Phase 2 plots with one Phase 3 plot for about every 95,000 acres. Phase 3 measurements are obtained by field crews during the growing season and include an extended suite of ecological data: lichen diversity and abundance, soil quality (erosion, compaction, and chemistry), vegetation diversity and structure, and down woody material. The incidence and severity of ozone injury for selected bioindicator species also are monitored as part of an associated sampling scheme. All Phase 2 measurements are collected on each Phase 3 plot at the same time as the Phase 3 measurements. Additional information on data-collection procedures used in Phase 3 is available at http://www.nrs.fs.fed.us/fia/topics/.

Phase 3 variables are selected to address specific criteria outlined by the Montreal Process Working Group for the conservation and sustainable management of temperate and boreal forests (Montreal Process 1995) and are based on the concept of indicator variables. Observations of an indicator variable represent an index of ecosystem functions that can be monitored over time to assess trends. Indicator variables are used in conjunction with each other, Phase 2 data, data from FHM evaluation monitoring studies, and ancillary data to address ecological issues such as vegetation diversity, fuel loading, regional air-quality gradients, and carbon storage. The Phase 2 and 3 data of the enhanced FIA program are a primary source of reporting data for the Montreal Process Criteria.

## Estimation

Most of the estimates and analysis of forest resources in this report, including the estimates in Tables 1-20, 31-32, 54-59a, and 65 are based on data collected on the 8,302 Phase 2 plots across South Dakota (Fig. 2). The analysis of forest health issues that relate to down woody materials, soils, ozone damage, and crown condition are based on data collected on the 520 Phase 3 plots (Fig 3). Data from Phase 3 plots is used in generating crown Tables 66 through 69.

Figure 2. Approximate location of forest land (green dots) and nonforest land (yellow dots) Phase 2 plots, South Dakota, 2005.

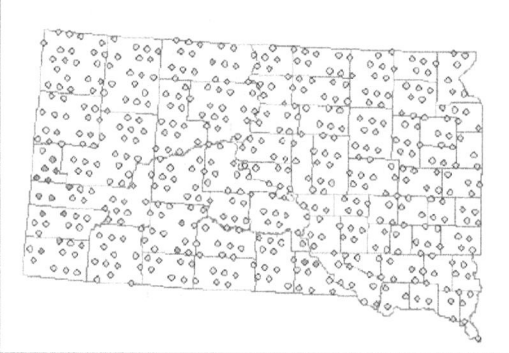

Figure 3. Approximate location of forest land (green dots) and nonforest land (yellow dots) Phase 3 plots, South Dakota, 2005.

About 20 percent of the Phase 2 observations were acquired each year from October 1, 2000 to September 30, 2005. These observations, collectively called the 2005 inventory, are within 28 estimation strata (Table A) defined by combinations of the four Phase 1 classes (nonforest, nonforest edge, forest edge, and forest), a land-ownership classification created from the PAD and forest-survey units. Procedures described in Bechtold and Patterson (2005) for stratified estimation with observed stratum areas were used in conjunction with the strata in Table A to produce all estimates. The total area and number of plots within each stratum is shown in Table A.

## Integration with Previous Inventories

In 2005, FIA completed measurement of the fifth panel of inventory plots in South Dakota. The 2005 panel, along with those surveyed in 2001, 2002, 2003, and 2004, comprise the dataset for the fifth inventory of South Dakota's forests (Piva et al. 2009). The first inventory of South Dakota was completed in 1935 (Ware 1936). The second inventory is dated 1962 [all lands west of the 103rd meridian were inventoried in 1960 (Choate and Spencer 1969) and east of the 103rd meridian were inventoried in 1964 (Chase 1967). The third inventory is dated 1984 [all lands east of the 103rd meridian were inventoried in 1979 (Raile 1984) and west of the 103rd meridian were inventoried in 1983 (Collins and Green 1988, 1989)]. The fourth inventory is dated 1996 [the area outside the Black Hills National Forest was inventoried in 1996 (Leatherberry et al. 2000) and the Black Hills National Forest was inventoried in 1999 (DeBlander 2002)]. A partial inventory of South Dakota (all lands west of the 103rd meridian) was conducted from 1971 to 1974 (Green 1978), but land to the east of the 103rd meridian was not inventoried.

Data from new inventories often are compared with data from earlier inventories to determine trends in forest resources. However, for the comparisons to be valid, the procedures used in the two inventories must be similar. As a result of our ongoing efforts to improve the efficiency and reliability of the inventory there have been several changes in procedures and definitions since the 1996 South Dakota inventory. These changes will have little impact on statewide estimates of forest area, timber volume, and tree biomass but they may significantly affect condition-classification variables such as forest type and stand-size class.

For consistency, a new, national plot design was implemented by all five regional FIA units in 1999 in which fixed-radius subplots are used exclusively. Prior to this new plot design (during the 1984 and 1996 inventories), fixed and variable-radius subplots were used. Both designs have strong points but they often produce different classifications for condition characteristics. Procedures for assigning condition attributes such as forest type, stand age, and stocking changed significantly with the introduction of the new annual plot design. However, FIA research (unpublished) comparing these plot designs, showed no noticeable difference in volume and tree-count estimates.

For additional information on the sample protocols and estimation procedures for the first two phases of the FIA program, see Bechtold and Patterson (2005). For additional information on Phase 3 indicator sampling protocols, see USDA Forest Service (2003) and Woodall and Monleon (2008).

## QUALITY OF THE ESTIMATES

Two general types of error – random variability (precision) and estimation bias (accuracy) – are of interest to users. Random variability refers to the precision of the estimate, which would occur if the entire sampling and estimation process were repeated many times. Estimation bias refers to the difference between the estimate and the "true value" in the absence of this random variability, and to the overestimation or underestimation inherent in the entire estimation process.

Errors in the estimates in this report (both random variability and estimation bias) are affected by various sources. The four primary sources of error common to all sample-based estimates are sampling, measurement, prediction, and nonresponse error. The following sections provide a definition for each source of error in the context of the FIA inventory as well as a discussion of methods used to quantify and/or reduce that source of error. Measures of sampling, measurement, and prediction errors associated with various attributes are presented. Issues of possible bias related to nonresponse also are addressed.

# Sampling Error

The process of sampling (selecting a random subset of a population and calculating estimates from this subset) causes estimates to contain error they would not have if every member of the population (e.g., every tree in South Dakota) had been observed and included in the sample. The 2005 State inventory is based on a sample of 8,302 plots located randomly across South Dakota (total area of 49.4 million acres), or a sampling rate of about one plot for every 5,945 acres

The procedures for statistical estimation outlined in the previous section and described in detail in Bechtold and Patterson (2005) provide the estimates of the population totals and means in this report. Along with every estimate is an associated sampling error that is typically expressed as a percentage of the estimated value (the estimated value plus or minus the sampling error). This sampling error is the primary measure of the reliability of an estimate. We use a sampling error based on one standard error, that is, the chances are two in three that the results would have been within the limits indicated had a 100-percent inventory been conducted using these methods.

Sampling errors for State-level estimates of the major attributes presented in this report are in Table B. Table 65 presents includes errors for these estimates at the county-group level (counties assigned to each group are listed in the footnote).

Estimates for classifications smaller than the State totals in Table B have larger sampling errors. For example, Table 65 shows that the sampling error for timberland area in any county is higher than that for total timberland area in South Dakota. To compute an approximate sampling error for an estimate that is smaller than a State total, use the following formula:

$$E = \frac{(SE)\sqrt{(\text{State total estimate})}}{\sqrt{(\text{Smaller estimate})}} \qquad (1)$$

where:

  $E$ = approximate sampling error for smaller estimate
  $SE$ = sampling error for State total estimate (percent)

For example, to compute the error on the area of forest land in the oak/hickory forest-type group for the State, proceed as follows:

The total area of the ponderosa pine group in the State (from Table 3) is 1,137,500 acres.

The total area of all forest land in the State (from Table 3) is 1,682,100 acres.

The State total error for forest-land area (from Table B) is 3.33 percent.

Using formula (1):

Sampling error = $E = (3.33)\sqrt{1682100} / \sqrt{1137500} = 4.05$ percent.

This approximation works well for estimates of area, volume, number of trees, and biomass. Individuals seeking more accurate sampling errors should use the estimation tools available at www.fia.fs.fed.us/tools-data/.

The estimators used by FIA are unbiased under the assumptions that the sample plots are a random sample of the total population, and that the observed value for any plot is the true value for that plot. Deviations from these basic assumptions are not reflected in the computation of sampling errors. The following sections on measurement, prediction, and nonresponse error address possible departures from these basic assumptions.

## Measurement Error

Errors associated with the methods and instruments used to observe and record the sample attributes are called measurement errors. On FIA plots, attributes such as the diameter and height of a tree are measured with different instruments; other attributes such as species and crown class are observed without the aid of an instrument. On a typical FIA plot, 15 to 50 trees are observed with 15 to 20 attributes recorded on each tree. Also, many attributes that describe the plot and conditions on the plot are observed. Errors in any of these observations affect the quality of the estimates. If a measurement is biased (such as tree diameter consistently taken at an incorrect place on the tree) the estimates that use this observation (such as volume) will reflect this bias.

To ensure that all FIA observations are made to the highest standards possible, a regular program of quality control and quality assurance is an integral part of all FIA data-collection efforts. This program begins with the documentation of protocols and procedures used in the inventory followed by extensive crew training. To assess the quality of the data collected by these trained crews, a random sample of at least 4 percent of all plots is measured independently by a different qualified crew. These independent measurements are called blind checks. A second measurement on blind-check plots is made by a quality assurance (QA) crew. QA crews have as much or more experience and training in FIA field measurements as that of a standard FIA crew.

The quality of field measurements is assessed nationally through a set of measurement quality objectives (MQOs) that are set for every data item collected. Each MQO consists of two parts: a tolerance or acceptable level of measurement error and an objective in terms of the percentage of measurements within tolerance. Blind check measurements are used to observe how often individual field crews are meeting these objectives and to assess the overall compliance among all crews. Table C shows the compliance rates for various measurements used to compute the estimates included in this and other FIA reports. The column labeled "South Dakota" is based on blind check measurements of plots used in this report. The column labeled "Plains States" come from all measurements by FIA crews within North Dakota, South Dakota, Nebraska, and Kansas. The column labeled "North Central States" comes from measurements by FIA crews within an 11-state area (Illinois, Indiana, Iowa, Kansas, Michigan, Minnesota, Missouri, Nebraska, North Dakota, South Dakota, and Wisconsin). Training and supervision of crews is a regional effort and crews often work in more than one state. Regional data-quality observations reflect the overall measurement quality of all data collected by FIA in the Northern States.

In South Dakota, many variables such as d.b.h. have a low tolerance (± 0.1 inch) and a high percentage of data within the tolerance (76.6 percent). Measurements for determining tree-size class are precise. By contrast, variables such as stand age have a larger tolerance (± 10 years) and fewer data within the tolerance (37.9 percent). The estimate of stand age is based on the composition of all age classes within a stand. Often a stand is heterogeneous by age but a single value must be assigned to it. This can confound analysis of stand age over time.

Blind check observations also were used to test for relative bias in the field-crew measurements. Relative bias is defined here as a tendency for standard measurements by field-crews to be higher or lower than measurements by QA crews. The estimated relative bias and limits of 95-percent confidence intervals (based on parametric bootstrap estimates) for the relative bias are presented in Table D. Relative bias is reported only for variables that are measurements of continuous attributes (e.g., diameter and height) and several coded variables that are ordinal in nature (e.g., crown position). Relative bias is not appropriate for most coded variables.

Blind check measurements do not provide direct observations of true bias in field measurements (average difference between field measurements and true values) because they are paired observations of two field measurements. The QA crew in these blind checks typically has more training and experience with FIA field measurements than the first crew, but both crews use the same methods and instruments to obtain measurements. These methods have been identified as the best available and selected for nationwide use by FIA, and are commonly used by similar natural-resource inventories. A basic assumption is that when applied correctly, these methods provide unbiased observations of the attribute they are designed to measure. Under this assumption, relative bias observations in Table D provide observations of bias due to the difference in experience and training between the field and QA crews. In most cases, there is no significant bias.

## Prediction Error

Errors associated with mathematical models (such as volume models) aimed at providing observations of the attributes of interest based on sample attributes are called prediction errors. Area, number of trees, volume, biomass, growth, removals, and mortality are the primary attributes of interest in this report. Estimates of area and number of trees are based on direct observation and do not rely on prediction models. Models are used to predict volume and biomass estimates for individual trees. Change estimates such as growth, mortality, and removals are based on these model-based predictions of volume from both the current plot measurements and the measurements taken in the previous inventory.

Estimates of prediction errors associated with volume models used in this report are presented by Hahn and Hansen (1991) along with the model forms, methods used in model development, and model-parameter estimates. The estimated prediction errors are based on observations of 10,453 trees measured in the 1989 Missouri inventory (Spencer et al. 1992). For gross cubic-foot volume in live trees, there was a 2.5 percent overprediction across all species, an underprediction of 4.3 percent in trees less than 10 inches in d.b.h., and an overprediction of 7.1 in trees 20 inches and larger in d.b.h. Prediction errors were similar for board foot estimates.

In comparing FIA estimates with those from other data sources, users should be aware of the prediction models used in both estimates. If both estimates are based on the same prediction models with matching fitted-parameter values, the prediction bias of one estimate should cancel out that of the other estimate. If the estimates are based on different prediction models, the prediction error of both models must be considered.

# Nonresponse Error

Nonresponse error occurs when crews are unable to measure a plot (or a portion of a plot) at a selected location. Nonresponse falls into three classes:

- Denied access – Entire plots or portions of plots where the field crew is unable to obtain permission from the landowner to measure trees on the plot.
- Hazardous/inaccessible – Entire plots or portions of plots where conditions prevent a crew from safely accessing the plot or measuring trees on the plot.
- Other – Plots on which the field crew is unable to obtain a valid measurement for reasons other than those stated.

Nonresponse has two effects on the sample: it reduces the sample size, which is reflected in the sampling errors, and it can bias the estimates if the portion of the population not being sampled differs from the portion being sampled.

In FIA, nonresponse rates are relatively low. In the 2005 South Dakota inventory, 8,302 sample plots were selected for observation. All but 20 of these plots were included in the sample used to estimate current resources. On 14 plots, crews were unable to obtain owner permission to measure the plot or part of the plot; hazardous conditions on six plots prevented the crew from measuring all or part of the plot.

Even an overall nonresponse rate of 1 percent can cause considerable bias if not properly accounted for. The major source of nonresponse is denied access to plots, which occurs primarily on lands in private ownership. Also, observations for plots on nonforest and water land classes rarely require crews to physically enter the land. Nor is permission needed because the observation can be obtained from aerial photos or other sources of remotely sensed information.

The stratified estimation process used by FIA with strata defined by two ownership classes (private and public) and four Landsat TM forest cover classes (nonforest, nonforest edge, forest edge, and forest) reduces the possible effects of bias caused by nonresponse. Under the stratified estimation process used by FIA, nonresponses are removed from the sample, and stratum estimates (means, totals, and sampling errors) are obtained only from plots with valid observations. The net effect in the estimates of means and totals is that the average of the observed plots within the stratum (ownership-forest-cover class) becomes the estimate for all nonresponses within that stratum. The nonresponse rate in one stratum does not affect the estimate in other strata. The response rate within each stratum for the South Dakota 2005 inventory is presented in Table A.

In Table 1 of this report, we acknowledge denied access and hazardous as two land classes in South Dakota within which we are unable to provide estimates on variables such as forest area and timber volume. However, we do report the total estimated area in each of these classes. In all other tables of this report, we do not acknowledge either of these classes, and in the estimation process we treat the sample where we do have observations as a random sample of the entire State.

The nonresponse plots in this inventory were not permanently removed from the FIA system of plots. We will attempt to measure these plots in future inventories. At that time we may be able to obtain permission to access these plots, hazardous conditions may have changed, and/or other circumstances that caused us to drop plots from a specific inventory cycle may well change.

## GLOSSARY

**Average annual mortality:** The average annual change in mortality of trees during the period between inventories. This estimate can be provided in cubic feet for live and growing-stock trees that died or in board feet for sawtimber trees that died.

**Average annual net growth:** The average annual change in the volume of trees during the period between inventories. Components include the change in volume of trees that have met the minimum size requirements over the inventory period, plus the volume of trees reaching the minimum size during the period (ingrowth), minus the volume of trees that died during the period, minus the volume of cull during the period. Mortality removals (trees killed in the harvesting process and left on site) and diversion removals (trees removed from the forest-land base due to a change from forest to nonforest land) are not included. This estimate can be provided in cubic feet for live and growing-stock trees or in board feet for sawtimber trees.

**Average annual removals:** The average annual change in removals of trees during the period between inventories. The estimate includes harvest removals, mortality removals (trees killed in the harvesting process and left on site), and diversion removals (trees removed from the forest-land base due to a change from forest to nonforest land). This estimate can be provided in cubic feet for live and growing-stock trees or in board feet for sawtimber trees.

**Basal area:** Tree area in square feet of the cross section at breast height of a single tree. When the basal areas of all trees in a stand are summed, the result usually is expressed as square feet of basal area per acre.

**Bioindicator species:** A tree, woody shrub, or herb species that responds to ambient levels of ozone pollution with distinct visible foliar symptoms that are easy to diagnose.

**Biomass:** The aboveground volume of live trees (including bark but excluding foliage) reported in dry tons (dry weight). Biomass has four components:

*Bole:* Biomass of a tree from 1 foot above the ground to a 4-inch top outside bark or to a point where the central stem breaks into limbs.

*Tops and limbs:* Total biomass of a tree from a 1-foot stump minus the bole.

*1-to 5-inch trees:* Total aboveground biomass of a tree from 1 to 5 inches in d.b.h.

*Stump:* Biomass of a tree 5 inches d.b.h. and larger from the ground to a height of 1 foot.

**Bulk density:** The mass of soil per unit volume. A measure of the ratio of pore space to solid materials in a given soil. It is expressed in units of grams per cubic centimeter of oven dry soil.

**Coarse woody debris (CWD):** Dead branches, twigs, and wood splinters 3.0 inches in diameter and larger measured at the smallest end.

**Commercial species:** Tree species suitable for industrial wood products.

**Compacted live crown ratio:** The percent of the total length of the tree that supports a full, live crown. To determine compacted live crown ratio for trees that have uneven length crowns, lower branches are visually transferred to fill holes in the upper portions of the crown, until a full, even crown is created.

**Corporate:** An ownership class of private lands owned by corporations.

**County and municipal:** An ownership class of public lands owned by counties or local public agencies, or lands leased by these governmental units for more than 50 years. Also known as local government.

**Cropland:** Land under cultivation within the last 24 months, including cropland harvested, crop failures, cultivated summer fallow, idle cropland used only for pasture, orchards, active Christmas tree plantations indicated by annual shearing, nurseries, and land in soil improvement crops but excluding land cultivated in developing improved pasture.

**Crown:** The part of a tree or woody plant bearing live branches or foliage.

**Crown dieback:** Recent mortality of branches with fine twigs, which begins at the terminal portion of a branch and proceeds toward the trunk. Dieback is considered only when it occurs in the upper and outer portions of the tree. When whole branches are dead in the upper crown, without obvious signs of damage such as breaks or animal injury, it is assumed the branches died from the terminal portion of the branch. Dead branches in the lower portion of the live crown are assumed to have died from competition and shading.

**Cull tree:** A live tree, 5.0 inches in d.b.h. or larger, that is unmerchantable for saw logs now or prospectively because of rot, roughness, or species (see definitions for rotten and rough trees).

**Decay class:** Qualitative assessment of stage of decay (5 classes) of coarse woody debris based on visual assessments of color of wood, presence/absence of twigs and branches, texture of rotten portions, and structural integrity.

**Diameter class:** A classification of trees based on diameter outside bark measured at breast height (4-1/2 feet above ground). D.b.h. is the common abbreviation for "diameter at breast height." With 2-inch diameter classes, the 6-inch class, for example, includes trees 5.0 through 6.9 inches d.b.h. A "diameter at root collar" or d.r.c. measurement is acquired for multi-stemmed woodland species (e.g., Rocky Mountain juniper).

**Down woody material (DWM):** Woody pieces of trees and shrubs that have been uprooted (no longer supporting growth) or severed from their root system, not self-supporting, and lying on the ground.

**Duff:** A soil layer dominated by organic material derived from the decomposition of plant and animal litter and deposited on either an organic or a mineral surface. This layer is distinguished from the litter layer in that the original organic material has undergone sufficient decomposition that the source of this material (e.g., individual plant parts) no longer can be identified.

**Effective cation exchange capacity (ECEC):** The sum of cations that a soil can adsorb in its natural pH. It is expressed in units of centimoles of positive charge per kilogram of soil.

**Federal:** An ownership class of public lands owned by the U.S. Government.

**Fiber products:** Products derived from wood and bark residues, such as pulp, composition board products, and wood chips.

**Fine materials:** Wood residues not suitable for chipping, such as planer shavings and sawdust.

**Fine woody debris (FWD):** Dead branches, twigs, and wood splinters 0.1 to 2.9 inches in diameter.

**Forest land:** Land at least 10-percent stocked by trees of any size, including land that formerly had such tree cover and that will be naturally or artificially regenerated. Forest land includes transition zones, such as areas between heavily forested and nonforested lands that are at least 10-percent stocked with trees and forest areas adjacent to urban and builtup lands. Also included are pinyon-juniper and chaparral areas in the West and afforested areas. The minimum area for classification of forest land is 1 acre and 120 feet wide measured stem-to-stem from the outer-most edge. Unimproved roads and trails, streams, and clearings in forest areas are classified as forest if less than 120 feet wide.

**Forest type:** A classification of forest land based on the species presently forming a plurality of the live-tree stocking. If softwoods predominate (50 percent or more), then the forest type will be one of the softwood types and vice versa for hardwoods. For the Eastern United States, there are mixed hardwood-pine forest types when the pine and/or redcedar (either eastern or southern) component is between 25 and 49 percent of the stocking. If the pine/redcedar component is less than 25 percent of the stocking, then one of the hardwood forest types is assigned.

**Forest-type group:** Combinations of forest types that share closely associated species or site requirements and are generally combined for brevity of reporting. See forest type for examples of forest-type group members.

**Growing stock:** A classification of timber inventory that includes live trees of commercial species meeting specified standards of quality or vigor. Rough and rotten cull trees are excluded. When associated with volume, this includes only trees 5.0 inches d.b.h. and larger.

**Hardwood:** A dicotyledonous tree, usually broad-leaved and deciduous.

    *Soft hardwoods:* A category of hardwood species with wood generally of low specific gravity (less than 0.5). Notable examples include red maple, paper birch, quaking aspen, and American elm.

    *Hard hardwoods:* A category of hardwood species with wood generally of high specific gravity (greater than 0.5). Notable examples include sugar maple, yellow birch, black walnut, and oaks.

**Industrial wood:** All commercial roundwood products except fuelwood.

**Land area:** The area of dry land and land temporarily or partly covered by water, such as marshes, swamps, and river flood plains; streams, sloughs, estuaries, and canals less than 200 feet wide; and lakes, reservoirs, and ponds less than 4.5 acres in area.

**Litter:** Undecomposed or only partially decomposed organic material that can be readily identified (e.g., plant leaves, twigs).

**Live cull:** A classification that includes live, cull trees. When associated with volume, it is the net volume in live, cull trees that are 5.0 inches d.b.h. and larger.

**Local government:** An ownership class of public lands owned by counties or local public agencies, or lands leased by these governmental units for more than 50 years. Also known as county and municipal.

**Logging residues:** The unused portions of growing-stock and nongrowing-stock trees cut or killed by logging and left in the woods.

**Merchantable:** Refers to a pulpwood or saw log section that meets pulpwood or saw log specifications, respectively.

**National Forest:** An ownership class of Federal lands, designated by executive order or statute as National Forests or purchase units, and other lands under the administration of the Forest Service, including experimental areas.

**Net volume in cubic feet:** The gross volume in cubic feet less deductions for rot, roughness, and poor form. Volume is computed for the central stem from a 1-foot stump to a minimum 4.0-inch top diameter outside bark, or to the point where the central stem breaks into limbs.

**Noncommercial species:** Tree species of typically small size, poor form, or inferior quality, which normally do not develop into trees suitable for industrial wood products.

**Noncorporate private:** Nongovernmental conservation and natural resource organizations; unincorporated local partnerships, associations, and clubs; and Native American communities.

**Nonforest land:** Land that has never supported forests and lands formerly forested where use of timber management is precluded by development for other uses. (Note: Includes area used for crops, improved pasture, residential areas, city parks, improved roads of any width and adjoining clearings, powerline clearings of any width, and 1- to 4.5-acre areas of water classified by the Bureau of the Census as land. If intermingled in forest areas, unimproved roads and nonforest strips must be more than 120 feet wide, and clearings, etc., must be more than 1 acre in area to qualify as nonforest land.)

**Nonstocked areas:** Timberland less than 10-percent stocked with live trees.

**Other red oaks:** A group of species in the genus *Quercus* that includes scarlet oak, northern pin oak, southern red oak, bear oak, shingle oak, laurel oak, blackjack oak, water oak, pin oak, willow oak, and black oak.

**Other white oaks:** A group of species in the genus *Quercus* that includes overcup oak, chestnut oak, and post oak.

**Ownership:** The property owned by one ownership unit.

**Ownership unit:** A classification of ownership encompassing all types of legal entities having an ownership interest in land, regardless of the number of people involved. A unit may be an individual, a combination of persons; a legal entity such as a corporation, partnership, club, or trust, or a public agency. An ownership unit has control of a parcel or group of parcels of land.

**Ozone:** A regional, gaseous air pollutant produced primarily through sunlight-driven chemical reactions of nitrogen dioxide and hydrocarbons in the atmosphere and causing foliar injury to deciduous trees, conifers, shrubs, and herbaceous species.

**Ozone bioindicator site:** An open area used for ozone injury evaluations on ozone-sensitive species. The area must meet certain site selection guidelines on size, condition, and plant counts to be used for ozone injury evaluations in FIA.

**Physiographic class:** A measure of soil and water conditions that affect tree growth on a site. The physiographic classes are as follows:

**Xeric:** Very dry soils where excessive drainage seriously limits both growth and species occurrence. These sites are usually on upland and upper half slopes.

**Xeromesic:** Moderately dry soils where excessive drainage limits growth and species occurrence to some extent. These sites are usually on the lower half slopes.

**Mesic:** Deep, well-drained soils. Growth and species occurrence are limited only by climate. These include all cove sites (small sheltered bays) and bottomlands (low land) along intermittent streams.

**Hydromesic:** Moderately wet soils where insufficient drainage or infrequent flooding limits growth and species occurrence to some extent.

**Hydric:** Very wet sites where excess water seriously limits both growth and species occurrence.

**Poletimber trees:** Live trees at least 5.0 inches in d.b.h. but smaller than sawtimber trees.

**Primary wood-using mill:** A mill that converts roundwood products into other wood products. Common examples are sawmills that convert saw logs into lumber and pulpmills that convert pulpwood into wood pulp.

**Productivity class:** A classification of forest land in terms of potential annual cubic-foot volume growth per acre at culmination of mean annual increment in fully stocked natural stands.

**Pulpwood:** Roundwood, whole-tree chips, or wood residues used for the production of wood pulp.

**Reserved forest land:** Forest land withdrawn from timber utilization through statute, administrative regulation, or designation without regard to productive status.

**Residues:** Bark and woody materials that are generated in primary wood-using mills when roundwood products are converted to other products. Examples include slabs, edgings, trimmings, miscuts, sawdust, shavings, veneer cores and clippings, and pulp screenings. Includes bark residues and wood residues (both coarse and fine materials) but excludes logging residues.

**Rotten tree:** A live tree of commercial species that does not contain a saw log now or prospectively primarily because of rot (that is, when rot accounts for more than 50 percent of the total cull volume).

**Rough tree:** (a) A live tree of commercial species that does not contain a saw log now or prospectively primarily because of roughness (that is, when sound cull due to such factors as poor form, splits, or cracks accounts for more than 50 percent of the total cull volume) or (b) a live tree of noncommercial species.

**Roundwood products:** Logs, bolts, and other round timber generated from harvesting trees for industrial or consumer use.

**Salvable dead tree:** A downed or standing dead tree considered currently or potentially merchantable by regional standards.

**Saplings:** Live trees 1.0 inch through 4.9 inches d.b.h.

**Saw log:** A log meeting minimum standards of diameter, length, and defect, including logs at least 8 feet long, sound and straight, and with a minimum diameter inside bark of 6 inches for softwoods and 8 inches for hardwoods, or meeting other combinations of size and defect specified by regional standards.

**Sawtimber tree:** A live tree of commercial species containing at least a 12-foot saw log or two noncontiguous saw logs 8 feet or longer, and meeting regional specifications for freedom from defect. Softwoods must be at least 9.0 inches d.b.h. Hardwoods must be at least 11.0 inches d.b.h.

**Sawtimber volume:** Net volume of the saw log portion of live sawtimber in board feet, International 1/4-inch rule (unless specified otherwise), from stump to a minimum 7.0 inches top d.o.b. for softwoods and a minimum 9.0 inches top d.o.b. for hardwoods.

**Seedlings:** Live trees less than 1.0 inch d.b.h. and at least 1 foot in height.

**Select red oaks:** A group of species in the genus *Quercus* that includes cherrybark oak, northern red oak, and Shumard oak.

**Select white oaks:** A group of species in the genus *Quercus* that includes white oak, swamp white oak, bur oak, swamp chestnut oak, and chinkapin oak.

**Site index:** An expression of forest site quality based on the height of a free-growing dominant or codominant tree of a representative species in the forest type at age 50.

**Snag:** A standing dead tree. In the current inventory, a snag must be 5.0 inches d.b.h./d.r.c. and 4.5 feet tall, and have a lean angle less than 45 degrees from vertical. A snag may be either self-supported by its roots, or supported by another tree or snag.

**Softwood:** A coniferous tree, usually evergreen, having needles or scale-like leaves.

**Soil order:** The broadest category or class of soil based largely on the processes that formed the soil as indicated by the presence or absence of diagnostic horizons or layers.

**Sound dead:** The net volume in salvable dead trees.

**Stand:** A group of trees on a minimum of 1 acre of forest land that is stocked by forest trees of any size.

**Stand-size class:** A classification of forest land based on the size class of live trees in the area. The classes are as follows:

*Nonstocked:* Forest land stocked with less than 10 percent of full stocking with live trees. Examples are recently cutover areas or recently reverted agricultural fields.

*Seedling-sapling:* Forest land stocked with at least 10 percent of full stocking with live trees with half or more of such stocking in seedlings or saplings or both.

*Poletimber:* Forest land stocked with at least 10 percent of full stocking with live trees with half or more of such stocking in poletimber or sawtimber trees or both, and in which the stocking of poletimber exceeds that of sawtimber.

*Sawtimber:* Forest land stocked with at least 10 percent of full stocking with live trees with half or more of such stocking in poletimber or sawtimber trees or both, and in which the stocking of sawtimber is at least equal to that of poletimber.

**State:** An ownership class of public lands owned by states or lands leased by states for more than 50 years. Also a general reference to one of the political and geographic subdivisions of the United States.

**Stocking:** The degree of occupancy of land by trees, measured by basal area or number of trees by size and spacing, or both, compared to a stocking standard; that is, the basal area or number of trees, or both, required to fully utilize the growth potential of the land.

**Timberland:** Forest land that is producing or is capable of producing crops of industrial wood and not withdrawn from timber utilization by statute or administrative regulation. (Note: Areas qualifying as timberland are capable of producing in excess of 20 cubic feet per acre per year of industrial wood in natural stands. Currently inaccessible and inoperable areas are included.)

**Timber products output:** All timber products cut from roundwood and byproducts of wood manufacturing plants. Roundwood products include logs, bolts, or other round sections cut from growing-stock trees, cull trees, salvable dead trees, trees on nonforest land, noncommercial species, sapling-size trees, and limbwood. Byproducts from primary manufacturing plants include slabs, edging, trimmings, miscuts, sawdust, shavings, veneer cores and clippings, and screenings of pulpmills that are used as pulpwood chips or other products.

**Tree:** A woody plant usually having one or more erect perennial stems, a stem diameter at breast height of at least 3.0 inches, a more or less definitely formed crown of foliage, and a height of at least 15 feet at maturity.

**Tree size class:** A classification of trees based on diameter at breast height, including sawtimber trees, poletimber trees, saplings, and seedlings.

**Tops:** The wood of a tree above the merchantable height (or above the point on the stem 4.0 inches diameter outside bark (d.o.b.) or to the point where the central stem breaks into limbs). It includes the usable material in the uppermost stem.

**Urban forest land:** Land that would otherwise meet the criteria for timberland but is in an urban-suburban area surrounded by commercial, industrial, or residential development and not likely to be managed for the production of industrial wood products on a continuing basis. Wood removed would be for land clearing, fuelwood, or esthetic purposes. Such forest land may be associated with industrial, commercial, residential subdivision, industrial parks, golf course perimeters, airport buffer strips, and public urban parks that qualify as forest land.

**Unreserved forest land:** Forest land not withdrawn from harvest by statute or administrative regulation. This includes forest lands that are not capable of producing in excess of 20 cubic feet per acre per year of industrial wood in natural stands.

**Veneer log:** A roundwood product from which veneer is sliced or sawn and that usually meets certain standards of minimum diameter and length and maximum defect.

**Weight:** The weight of wood and bark, oven-dry basis (approximately 12 percent moisture content).

# LITERATURE CITED

Bechtold, W.A.; Patterson, P.L., eds. 2005. **The enhanced Forest Inventory and Analysis program—national sampling design and estimation procedures.** Gen. Tech. Rep. SRS-80. Asheville, NC: U.S. Department of Agriculture, Forest Service, Southern Research Station. 85 p.

Brand, G.J.; Nelson, M.D.; Wendt, D.G.; Nimerfro, K.K. 2000. **The hexagon/panel system for selecting FIA plots under an annual inventory.** In: McRoberts, R.E.; Reams, G.A.; Van Deusen, P.C., eds. Proceedings of the first annual Forest Inventory and Analysis symposium. Gen. Tech. Rep. NC-213. St. Paul, MN: U.S. Department of Agriculture, Forest Service, North Central Research Station: 8-13.

Chase, C.D. 1967. **Woodlands of eastern South Dakota.** St. Paul, MN: U.S. Department of Agriculture, Forest Service, North Central Forest Experiment Station. 38 p.

Choate, G.A.; Spencer, J.S. 1969. **Forests in South Dakota.** Resour. Bull. INT-8. Ogden, UT: U.S. Department of Agriculture, Forest Service, Intermountain Forest and Range Experiment Station. 40 p.

Collins, D.C.; Green, A.W. 1988. **South Dakota's timber resources.** Resour. Bull. INT-56. Ogden, UT: U.S. Department of Agriculture, Forest Service, Intermountain Research Station. 28 p.

Collins, D.C.; Green, A.W. 1989. **Western South Dakota: forest statistics for land outside National Forests, 1984.** Resour. Bull. INT-65. Ogden, UT: U.S. Department of Agriculture, Forest Service, Intermountain Research Station. 45 p.

DeBlander, L.T. 2002. **Forest resources of the Black Hills National Forest.** Ogden, UT: U.S. Department of Agriculture, Forest Service, Rocky Mountain Research Station. 13 p.

DellaSala, D.A.; Staus, N.L.; Strittholt, J.R.; Hackman, A.; Iacobelli, A. 2001. **An updated protected areas database for the United States and Canada.** Natural Areas Journal. 21(2): 124-135.

Green, A.W. 1978. **Timber resources of Western South Dakota.** Ogden, UT: U.S. Department of Agriculture, Forest Service, Intermountain Forest and Range Experiment Station. 56 p.

Hahn, J.T.; Hansen, M.H. 1991. **Cubic and board foot volume models for the Central States.** Northern Journal of Applied Forestry. 8: 47-57.

Hansen. M.H.; Wendt, D.G. 2000. **Using classified Landsat Thematic Mapper data for stratification in a statewide forest inventory.** In: McRoberts, R.E.; Reams, G.A.; Van Deusen, P.C., eds. Proceedings of the first annual Forest Inventory and Analysis symposium. Gen. Tech. Rep. NC-213. St. Paul, MN: U.S. Department of Agriculture, Forest Service, North Central Research Station.

Leatherberry, E.C.; Piva, R.J.; Josten, G.J. 2000. **South Dakota's forest resources outside the Black Hills National Forest, 1996.** Res. Pap. NC-338. St. Paul, MN: U.S. Department of Agriculture, Forest Service, North Central Research Station. 103 p.

McRoberts, R.E. 1999. **Joint annual forest inventory and monitoring system: the North Central perspective.** Journal of Forestry. 97: 21-26.

McRoberts, R.E.; Wendt, D.G.; Nelson, M.D.; Hansen, M.H. 2002. **Using a land cover classification based on satellite imagery to improve the precision of forest inventory area estimates.** Remote Sensing of the Environment. 80: 1-9.

McRoberts, R.E. 2005. **The enhanced forest inventory and analysis program.** In: Bechtold, W.A.; Patterson, P. L., eds. The enhanced forest inventory and analysis program–national sampling design and estimation procedures. Gen. Tech. Rep. SRS-80. Asheville, NC: U.S. Department of Agriculture, Forest Service, Southern Research Station: 1-10.

Montreal Process, 1995. **Criteria and indicators for the conservation and sustainable management of temperate and boreal forests.** Hull, PQ, Canada: Canadian Forest Service. 27 p.

Piva, R.J.; Moser, W.K.; Haugan, D.D.; Josten, G.J.; Brand, G.J.; Butler, B.J.; Crocker, S.J.; Hansen, M.H.; Meneguzzo, D.M.; Perry, C.H.; Woodall, C.W. 2009. **South Dakota's forests 2005.** Resour. Bull. NRS-35. Newtown Square, PA: U.S. Department of Agriculture, Forest Service, Northern Research Station. 96 p.

Raile, G.K. 1984. **Eastern South Dakota forest statistics,** 1980. Resour. Bull. NC-74. St. Paul, MN: U.S. Department of Agriculture, Forest Service, North Central Forest Experiment Station. 60 p.

USDA Forest Service. 2003. **Forest inventory and analysis national core field guide; Volume I: field data collection procedures for phase 2 plots, Volume II: Field data collection procedures for phase 3 plots.** Version 2.0. St. Paul, MN: U.S. Department of Agriculture, Forest Service, North Central Research Station. 410 p.

Vogelmann, J.E.; Howard, S.M.; Yang, L.; Larson, C.R.; Wylie, B.K.; Van Driel, N. 2001. **Completion of the 1990s National Land Cover Data Set for the conterminous United States from Landsat Thematic Mapper data and ancillary data sources.** Photogrammetric Engineering and Remote Sensing. 67: 650-662.

Ware, E.R. 1936. Forest of South Dakota. **Their economic importance and possibilities.** St. Paul, MN: U.S. Department of Agriculture, Forest Service, Lake States Forest Experiment Station. 28 p.

Woodall, C.W.; Monleon, V.J. 2008. **Sampling protocol, estimation, and analysis procedures for the down woody materials indicator of the FIA program.** Gen. Tech. Rep. NRS-22. Newtown Square, PA: U.S. Department of Agriculture, Forest Service, Northern Research Station. 68 p.

# TABLE TITLES

## Tables of Quality Assurance

Table A.—Area and number of plots in each stratum, South Dakota, 2005

Table B.—State-level estimates of major forest resource attributes and their sampling errors, South Dakota, 2005

Table C.—Percent compliance to measurement quality objectives (MQO) tolerances of variables for blind check plots, 2005

Table D.—Observed relative bias values (average [field crew – QA crew]) for measurement variables, blind check plots, 2005

## Tables of Estimation

Gaps in the enumeration of tables are placeholders for future reports.

**Area**

Table 1.—Percentage of area by land status, South Dakota, 2005

Table 2.—Area of forest land, in thousand acres, by owner class and forest-land status, South Dakota, 2005

Table 3.—Area of forest land, in thousand acres, by forest-type group and productivity class, South Dakota, 2005

Table 4.—Area of forest land, in thousand acres, by forest-type group, ownership group, and land status, South Dakota, 2005

Table 5.—Area of forest land, in thousand acres, by forest-type group and stand-size class, South Dakota, 2005

Table 6.—Area of forest land, in thousand acres, by forest-type group and stand-age class, South Dakota, 2005

Table 7.—Area of forest land, in thousand acres, by forest-type group and stand origin, South Dakota, 2005

Table 8.—Area of forest land, in thousand acres, by forest-type group and primary disturbance class, South Dakota, 2005

Table 9.—Area of timberland, in thousand acres, by forest-type group and stand-size class, South Dakota, 2005

## Number

Table 10.—Number of live trees, in thousands, on forest land by species group and diameter class, South Dakota, 2005

Table 11.—Number of growing-stock trees, in thousands, on timberland by species group and diameter class, South Dakota, 2005

## Volume

Table 12.—Net volume of all live trees, in million cubic feet, by owner class and forest-land status, South Dakota, 2005

Table 13.—Net volume of all live trees, in million cubic feet, on forest land by forest-type group and stand-size class, South Dakota, 2005

Table 13a.—Net volume of all live trees, in million cubic feet, on forest land by species and forest-type group, South Dakota, 2005

Table 14.—Net volume of all live trees, in million cubic feet, on forest land by species group and ownership group, South Dakota, 2005

Table 15.—Net volume of all live trees, in million cubic feet, on forest land by species group and diameter class, South Dakota, 2005

Table 16.—Net volume of all live trees, in million cubic feet, on forest land by forest-type group and stand origin, South Dakota, 2005

Table 17.—Net volume of growing-stock trees, in million cubic feet, on timberland by species group and diameter class, South Dakota , 2005

Table 18.—Net volume of growing-stock trees, in million cubic feet, on timberland by species group and ownership group, South Dakota, 2005

Table 19.—Net volume of sawtimber trees, in million board feet, (International 1/4-inch rule) on timberland by species group and diameter class, South Dakota, 2005

Table 19a.—Net volume of sawtimber trees, in million board feet, (Doyle rule) on timberland by species group and diameter class, South Dakota, 2005

Table 20.—Net volume of saw-log portion of sawtimber trees, in million cubic feet, on timberland by species group and ownership group, South Dakota, 2005

**Weight**

Table 31.—Live-tree aboveground dry weight, in thousand dry tons, (CRM) by owner class and forest-land status, South Dakota, 2005

Table 32.—Live-tree aboveground dry weight, in thousand dry tons, (CRM) on forest land by species group and diameter class, South Dakota, 2005

**County Level**

Table 54.—Area of accessible forest land, in thousand acres, by Forest Survey Unit, county, and forest-land status, South Dakota, 2005

Table 55.—Area of accessible forest land, in thousand acres, by Forest Survey Unit, county, ownership group and forest-land status, South Dakota, 2005

Table 56.—Area of forest land, in thousand acres, by Forest Survey Unit, county/county group, and forest-type group, South Dakota, 2005

Table 57.—Area of timberland, in thousand acres, by Forest Survey Unit, county, and stand-size class, South Dakota, 2005

Table 58.—Area of timberland, in thousand acres, by Forest Survey Unit, county, and stocking class, South Dakota, 2005

Table 59.—Net volume of growing-stock and sawtimber (International 1/4-inch rule) on timberland by Forest Survey Unit, county, and major species group, South Dakota, 2005

Table 59a.—Net volume of growing-stock and sawtimber (Doyle rule) on timberland by Forest Survey Unit, county, and major species group, South Dakota, 2005

Table 65.—Sampling errors by Forest Survey Unit and county for area of timberland, volume, average annual net growth, average annual removals, and average annual mortality on timberland, South Dakota, 2005

**Table A.—Area and number of plots in each stratum, South Dakota, 2005**

| County group[a] | Ownership layer[b] | Strata[c] | Area[d] (acres) | Selected[e] | Nonforest office plots[f] | Field check plots[g] | Field check plots measured[h] | Forest plots measured[i] | Denied access | Hazardous |
|---|---|---|---|---|---|---|---|---|---|---|
| Minnesota-Big Sioux-Coteau | Public and private | Forest and forest edge | 78,167 | 18 | 12 | 6 | 6 | 4 | - | - |
| Minnesota-Big Sioux-Coteau | Public and private | Nonforest | 7,902,011 | 1,318 | 1,300 | 18 | 17 | 8 | 1 | - |
| Minnesota-Big Sioux-Coteau | Public and private | Nonforest edge | 272,449 | 42 | 35 | 7 | 7 | 3 | - | - |
| NFS_108 (Custer National Forest) | Public | All | 73,960 | 13 | 8 | 5 | 5 | 4 | - | 1 |
| NFS_203 (Black Hills National Forest) | Public | Forest | 722,632 | 126 | - | 126 | 126 | 126 | - | - |
| NFS_203 (Black Hills National Forest) | Public | Forest edge | 195,391 | 35 | 1 | 34 | 34 | 34 | - | - |
| NFS_203 (Black Hills National Forest) | Public | Nonforest | 46,346 | 9 | 4 | 5 | 5 | 2 | - | - |
| NFS_203 (Black Hills National Forest) | Public | Nonforest edge | 106,806 | 18 | 3 | 15 | 15 | 13 | - | - |
| Bad-Missouri-Coteau-James | Private | Forest and forest edge | 184,227 | 32 | 13 | 19 | 19 | 15 | 1 | - |
| Bad-Missouri-Coteau-James | Private | Nonforest | 17,018,351 | 2,862 | 2,834 | 28 | 27 | 7 | 1 | - |
| Bad-Missouri-Coteau-James | Private | Nonforest edge | 392,752 | 77 | 63 | 14 | 14 | 7 | - | - |
| Belle Fourche-Grand-Moreau | Private | Forest | 134,183 | 22 | 11 | 11 | 11 | 11 | - | - |
| Belle Fourche-Grand-Moreau | Private | Forest edge | 787,023 | 132 | 123 | 9 | 9 | 7 | - | - |
| Belle Fourche-Grand-Moreau | Private | Nonforest | 5,993,175 | 998 | 991 | 7 | 6 | 2 | 1 | - |
| Belle Fourche-Grand-Moreau | Private | Nonforest edge | 1,291,189 | 228 | 218 | 10 | 10 | 5 | - | - |
| Cheyenne | Private | Forest | 98,557 | 23 | 8 | 15 | 13 | 12 | 1 | 1 |
| Cheyenne | Private | Forest edge | 347,634 | 57 | 41 | 16 | 12 | 11 | 4 | 2 |
| Cheyenne | Private | Nonforest | 5,996,907 | 1,013 | 991 | 22 | 19 | 6 | 3 | - |
| Cheyenne | Private | Nonforest edge | 634,941 | 103 | 88 | 15 | 14 | 8 | 1 | - |
| White-Niobrara | Private | Forest and forest edge | 105,067 | 11 | 3 | 8 | 7 | 7 | 1 | - |
| White-Niobrara | Private | Nonforest | 5,489,943 | 923 | 897 | 26 | 26 | 10 | - | - |
| White-Niobrara | Private | Nonforest edge | 205,284 | 39 | 19 | 20 | 18 | 15 | 1 | 2 |
| Bad-Missouri-Coteau-James | Public | All | 171,886 | 26 | 26 | - | - | - | - | - |
| Belle Fourche-Grand-Moreau | Public | All | 156,838 | 25 | 25 | - | - | - | - | - |
| Cheyenne | Public | Forest and forest edge | 54,175 | 8 | 4 | 4 | 4 | 4 | - | - |
| Cheyenne | Public | Nonforest | 590,099 | 88 | 88 | - | - | - | - | - |
| Cheyenne | Public | Nonforest edge | 39,196 | 9 | 4 | 5 | 5 | 4 | - | - |
| White-Niobrara | Public | All | 264,596 | 47 | 47 | - | - | - | - | - |
| Total | | | 49,353,785 | 8,302 | 7,857 | 445 | 429 | 325 | 14 | 6 |

**Continued**

25

**Table A.—continued**

**Table A—Footnote**

[a] County groups and counties.

| Belle Fourche-Grand-Moreau | | Bad-Missouri-Coteau-James | | Minnesota-Big Sioux-Coteau | | White-Niobrara |
|---|---|---|---|---|---|---|
| Butte | | Aurora | Hughes | Brookings | Roberts | Bennett |
| Corson | | Beadle | Hutchinson | Clark | Turner | Jackson |
| Dewey | | Bon Homme | Hyde | Clay | Union | Mellette |
| Harding | | Brown | Jerauld | Codington | | Shannon |
| Lawrence | | Brule | Jones | Day | | Todd |
| Perkins | | Buffalo | Lyman | Deuel | | Tripp |
| | | Campbell | McPherson | Grant | | |
| Cheyenne | | Charles Mix | Miner | Hamlin | | |
| Custer | | Davison | Potter | Kingsbury | | |
| Fall River | | Douglas | Sanborn | Lake | | |
| Haakon | | Edmunds | Spink | Lincoln | | |
| Meade | | Faulk | Stanley | Marshall | | |
| Pennington | | Gregory | Sully | McCook | | |
| Ziebach | | Hand | Walworth | Minnehaha | | |
| | | Hanson | Yankton | Moody | | |

[b] Ownership layer – Classification based on Protected Areas Database.

[c] Strata – Classification based on the 1992 NLCD classification and 2-pixel edge zones.

[d] Total area defined by intersection of ownership and classified NLCD layers within group of counties specified.

[e] Selected – Total number of plots selected to be sampled.

[f] Nonforest office plots – Selected plots whose observed classification as nonforest based on examination of aerial photographs and/or digital orthoquads.

[g] Field check plots – Selected plots that required field measurement.

[h] Field check plots measured – Field check plots where measurement was completed successfully. Excludes plots that were denied access, hazardous, or lost and measurement was not possible.

[i] Forest plots measured – Field check plots where forest condition was present on plot and measurement was completed in 2004 inventory. These plots are used to estimate current conditions, e.g., area, volume, number of trees, and biomass.

26

**Table B.—State-level estimates of major forest-resource attributes and their sampling errors, South Dakota, 2005**

| Item | State total | Sampling error |
|---|---|---|
| Growing stock on timberland | *thousand cubic feet* | *percent* |
| Volume | 1,898,216 | 5.21 |
| Sawtimber on timberland | *thousand board feet[a]* | |
| Volume | 6,580,386 | 6.58 |
| Area: | *acres* | |
| Forest land | 1,682,126 | 3.33 |
| Timberland | 1,541,319 | 3.62 |
| Biomass (aboveground live trees) | *thousand dry tons* | |
| Forest land | 42,706 | 4.88 |
| Timberland | 39,508 | 5.21 |

[a] International ¼-inch rule

Table C.—Percent compliance to measurement quality objectives (MQO) tolerances of variables for blind check plots, 2005

| Variable | Tolerance | Objective | South Dakota Data within tolerance | South Dakota Records | Plains States Data within tolerance | Plains States Records | North Central States Data within tolerance | North Central States Records |
|---|---|---|---|---|---|---|---|---|
| **Plot Level** | | | | | | | | |
| **National Variables** | | | | | | | | |
| Distance to Road | No Tolerance | 90.0% | 58.8% | 34 | 69.4% | 85 | 82.0% | 1,677 |
| Water on Plot | No Tolerance | 90.0% | 94.1% | 34 | 85.9% | 85 | 87.8% | 1,677 |
| **Regional Variables** | | | | | | | | |
| ELEVATION_GPS | ±50 ft | 99.0% | 74.2% | 31 | 72.2% | 79 | 83.0% | 1,528 |
| LAT_DECIMAL_DEG | ±0.0001 dg | 99.0% | 90.6% | 32 | 93.8% | 81 | 92.0% | 1,538 |
| LON_DECIMAL_DEG | ±0.0001 dg | 99.0% | 87.5% | 32 | 93.8% | 81 | 90.6% | 1,538 |
| LAT_FEET | ±140 ft | | 96.9% | 32 | 98.8% | 81 | 93.6% | 1,538 |
| LON_FEET | ±140 ft | | 93.8% | 32 | 97.5% | 81 | 97.7% | 1,538 |
| Results for | | | | 34 Plots | | 85 Plots | | 1,677 Plots |
| **Condition Level** | | | | | | | | |
| **National Variables** | | | | | | | | |
| Condition Status | No Tolerance | 99.0% | 98.5% | 66 | 98.2% | 217 | 99.0% | 2,595 |
| Reserve Status | No Tolerance | 99.0% | 98.5% | 66 | 98.6% | 217 | 99.4% | 2,595 |
| Owner Group | No Tolerance | 99.0% | 89.7% | 29 | 92.0% | 75 | 98.2% | 1,810 |
| Forest Type (Type) | No Tolerance | 95.0% | 86.2% | 29 | 70.7% | 75 | 82.7% | 1,810 |
| Forest Type (Group) | No Tolerance | 99.0% | 93.1% | 29 | 82.7% | 75 | 90.4% | 1,810 |
| Stand Size | No Tolerance | 99.0% | 86.2% | 29 | 73.3% | 75 | 87.0% | 1,810 |
| Regeneration Status | No Tolerance | 99.0% | 100.0% | 29 | 98.7% | 75 | 98.6% | 1,810 |
| Tree Density | No Tolerance | 99.0% | 93.1% | 29 | 92.0% | 75 | 96.9% | 1,810 |
| Owner Class | No Tolerance | 99.0% | 86.2% | 29 | 88.0% | 75 | 95.6% | 1,810 |
| Owner Status | No Tolerance | 99.0% | 100.0% | 29 | 100.0% | 75 | 98.0% | 1,810 |
| Regeneration Species | No Tolerance | 99.0% | 100.0% | 29 | 98.7% | 75 | 98.4% | 1,810 |
| Stand Age | ±10 % | 95.0% | 37.9% | 29 | 50.7% | 75 | 58.1% | 1,810 |
| Disturbance 1 | No Tolerance | 99.0% | 93.1% | 29 | 76.7% | 73 | 83.1% | 1,796 |
| Disturbance Year 1 | ±1 yr | 99.0% | 100.0% | 2 | 62.5% | 16 | 74.2% | 62 |
| Disturbance 2 | No Tolerance | 99.0% | 100.0% | 3 | 82.1% | 28 | 83.1% | 175 |
| Disturbance Year 2 | ±1 yr | 99.0% | . | . | 50.0% | 2 | 33.3% | 3 |
| Disturbance 3 | No Tolerance | 99.0% | . | . | 100.0% | 6 | 92.9% | 14 |
| Disturbance Year 3 | ±1 yr | 99.0% | . | . | . | . | . | . |
| Treatment 1 | No Tolerance | 99.0% | 82.8% | 29 | 86.3% | 73 | 95.2% | 1,796 |

**Continued**

**Table C.—continued**

| Variable | Tolerance | Objective | South Dakota Data within tolerance | Records | Plains States Data within tolerance | Records | North Central States Data within tolerance | Records |
|---|---|---|---|---|---|---|---|---|
| Treatment Year 1 | ±1 yr | 99.0% | 100.0% | 2 | 100.0% | 4 | 93.7% | 111 |
| Treatment 2 | No Tolerance | 99.0% | 100.0% | 7 | 100.0% | 14 | 90.8% | 195 |
| Treatment Year 2 | ±1 yr | 99.0% | . | . | . | . | 100.0% | 12 |
| Treatment 3 | No Tolerance | 99.0% | . | . | . | . | 100.0% | 29 |
| Treatment Year 3 | ±1 yr | 99.0% | . | . | . | . | 100.0% | 5 |
| Physiographic Class | No Tolerance | 80.0% | 51.7% | 29 | 61.3% | 75 | 77.1% | 1,810 |
| Present Nonforest Use | No Tolerance | 99.0% | 100.0% | 53 | 100.0% | 177 | 99.0% | 1,390 |
| Regional Variables | | | | | | | | |
| NC_LAND_USE | No Tolerance | 99.0% | 78.8% | 66 | 77.0% | 217 | 90.8% | 2,595 |
| Results for | | | 66 Conditions | | 217 Conditions | | 2,595 Conditions | |
| **Boundary Level** | | | | | | | | |
| National Variables | | | | | | | | |
| Boundary Change | No Tolerance | 99.0% | 100.0% | 5 | 100.0% | 18 | 90.3% | 421 |
| Constrasting Condition | No Tolerance | 99.0% | 80.0% | 5 | 77.8% | 18 | 91.9% | 421 |
| Left Azimuth | ±10 degrees | 90.0% | 40.0% | 5 | 55.6% | 18 | 84.1% | 421 |
| Corner Mapped | No Tolerance | 90.0% | 100.0% | 5 | 94.4% | 18 | 97.4% | 421 |
| Corner Azimuth | ±10 degrees | 90.0% | . | . | . | . | 70.6% | 17 |
| Corner Distance | ±1 ft | 90.0% | . | . | . | . | 70.6% | 17 |
| Right Azimuth | ±10 degrees | 90.0% | 20.0% | 5 | 44.4% | 18 | 84.3% | 421 |
| Results for | | | 5 Boundaries | | 18 Boundaries | | 421 Boundaries | |
| **Subplot Level** | | | | | | | | |
| National Variables | | | | | | | | |
| Subplot Center Cond | No Tolerance | 99.0% | 94.7% | 132 | 94.2% | 328 | 97.2% | 6,535 |
| Microplot Center Cond | No Tolerance | 99.0% | 93.9% | 132 | 93.6% | 328 | 96.8% | 6,535 |
| Slope | ±10 % | 90.0% | 85.6% | 132 | 88.7% | 328 | 97.6% | 6,535 |
| Aspect | ±10 ° | 90.0% | 76.7% | 116 | 77.4% | 287 | 88.6% | 6,021 |
| Snow/Water Depth | ±0.5 ft | | 94.7% | 132 | 94.2% | 328 | 66.8% | 6,535 |
| Results for | | | 132 Subplots | | 328 Subplots | | 6,535 Subplots | |

**Continued**

29

**Table C.—continued**

| | | | South Dakota | | Plains States | | North Central States | |
|---|---|---|---|---|---|---|---|---|
| Variable | Tolerance | Objective | Data within tolerance | Records | Data within tolerance | Records | Data within tolerance | Records |
| **Tree Level** | | | | | | | | |
| **National Variables** | | | | | | | | |
| DBH | ±0.1 /20 in. | 95.0% | 76.6% | 398 | 79.5% | 945 | 92.9% | 27,896 |
| DRC | ±0.1 /20 in. | 95.0% | . | . | 63.0% | 27 | 63.0% | 27 |
| Azimuth | ±10º | 90.0% | 96.0% | 398 | 97.5% | 972 | 98.8% | 27,923 |
| Horizontal Distance | ±0.2 /1.0 ft | 90.0% | 95.0% | 398 | 95.1% | 972 | 97.7% | 27,923 |
| Species | No Tolerance | 95.0% | 96.0% | 398 | 96.0% | 972 | 95.5% | 27,923 |
| Tree Genus | No Tolerance | 99.0% | 98.0% | 396 | 98.1% | 970 | 99.3% | 27,904 |
| Tree Status | No Tolerance | 95.0% | 99.7% | 398 | 99.6% | 972 | 99.0% | 27,923 |
| Rotten/Missing Cull | ±10 % | 90.0% | 99.0% | 299 | 96.9% | 813 | 98.9% | 18,782 |
| Total Length | ±10 % | 90.0% | 70.8% | 298 | 69.3% | 789 | 83.0% | 17,997 |
| Actual Length | ±10 % | 90.0% | 51.4% | 35 | 58.2% | 79 | 81.3% | 1,973 |
| Compacted Crown Ratio | ±10 % | 80.0% | 85.2% | 352 | 82.5% | 888 | 86.8% | 24,377 |
| Uncompacted Crown Ratio (P3) | ±10 % | 90.0% | 100.0% | 14 | 53.3% | 75 | 83.1% | 1,061 |
| Crown Class | No Tolerance | 85.0% | 71.3% | 352 | 69.9% | 888 | 83.0% | 24,377 |
| Decay Class | ±1 class | 90.0% | 67.4% | 46 | 76.7% | 86 | 95.4% | 2,860 |
| Cause of Death | No Tolerance | 80.0% | 91.3% | 46 | 95.3% | 86 | 92.2% | 2,860 |
| Condition | No Tolerance | 99.0% | 95.5% | 398 | 96.9% | 972 | 97.5% | 27,923 |
| Mortality Year | ±1 yr | 70.0% | 100.0% | 3 | 100.0% | 3 | 97.2% | 845 |
| Crown position | No Tolerance | | 92.9% | 14 | 53.3% | 75 | 33.4% | 850 |
| Crown light exposure | ±1 class | 85.0% | 92.9% | 14 | 68.0% | 75 | 32.6% | 1,061 |
| Sapling crown vigor class | No Tolerance | 85.0% | . | . | . | . | 73.0% | 211 |
| Crown density | ±10 % | 90.0% | 57.1% | 14 | 40.0% | 75 | 74.7% | 850 |
| Crown dieback | ±10 % | 90.0% | 100.0% | 14 | 94.7% | 75 | 97.2% | 850 |
| Transparency | ±10 % | 90.0% | 100.0% | 14 | 54.7% | 75 | 88.7% | 850 |
| **Regional Variables** | | | | | | | | |
| NC Tree Class | No Tolerance | 90.0% | 80.6% | 397 | 82.4% | 971 | 92.0% | 27,083 |
| NC Damage Agent 1 | No Tolerance | 90.0% | 88.9% | 352 | 83.4% | 888 | 92.5% | 24,377 |
| NC Damage Agent 2 | No Tolerance | 90.0% | 82.6% | 46 | 81.6% | 234 | 87.5% | 3,795 |
| Missouri damage code | No Tolerance | | . | . | . | . | 65.3% | 1,212 |
| Utilization | No Tolerance | 99.0% | 100.0% | 1 | 100.0% | 1 | 93.4% | 499 |

Continued

**Table C.—continued**

| Variable | Tolerance | Objective | South Dakota Data within tolerance | South Dakota Records | Plains States Data within tolerance | Plains States Records | North Central States Data within tolerance | North Central States Records |
|---|---|---|---|---|---|---|---|---|
| NC Tree Grade | No Tolerance | 90.0% | 75.5% | 147 | 63.9% | 241 | 68.8% | 4,502 |
| DBH-live & decay code 1-2 trees | ±0.1 /20 in. | 95.0% | 76.8% | 370 | 79.0% | 892 | 92.9% | 25,185 |
| DBH-decay code 3-4-5 trees | ±1 /20 in. | 95.0% | 72.7% | 11 | 91.7% | 36 | 98.9% | 1,133 |
| Total length trees 40 ft plus | ±10 % | 90.0% | 79.6% | 201 | 73.2% | 459 | 84.2% | 14,813 |
| Total length trees less than 40 ft | ±10 % | 90.0% | 52.6% | 97 | 63.9% | 330 | 77.2% | 3,184 |
| Total Length trees lt 5 inch | ±10 % | 90.0% | . | | 60.0% | 25 | 67.8% | 230 |
| Results for | | | | 398 Trees | | 972 Trees | | 27,923 Trees |
| **Seedling Level** | | | | | | | | |
| National Variables | | | | | | | | |
| Species | No Tolerance | 85.0% | 88.1% | 42 | 86.6% | 127 | 91.2% | 5,659 |
| Genus | No Tolerance | 90.0% | 100.0% | 42 | 92.1% | 127 | 96.9% | 5,659 |
| Seedling Count | ±20 % | 90.0% | 47.6% | 42 | 44.1% | 127 | 67.4% | 5,659 |
| Seedling Count coded | No Tolerance | 90.0% | 73.8% | 42 | 55.1% | 127 | 73.4% | 5,659 |
| Results for | | | | 32 Microplots | | 80 Microplots | | 2,402 Microplots |
| **Site Tree Level** | | | | | | | | |
| National Variables | | | | | | | | |
| Condition list | No Tolerance | 99.0% | 90.2% | 41 | 93.6% | 94 | 92.9% | 3,003 |
| Diameter | ±0.1 /20 in. | 95.0% | 65.9% | 41 | 75.5% | 94 | 89.4% | 2,870 |
| Species | No Tolerance | 95.0% | 100.0% | 41 | 98.9% | 94 | 97.0% | 3,003 |
| Genus | No Tolerance | 99.0% | 100.0% | 41 | 100.0% | 94 | 99.7% | 3,003 |
| Azimuth | ±10 degrees | 90.0% | 85.4% | 41 | 91.5% | 94 | 98.1% | 2,870 |
| Distance | ±5 feet | 90.0% | 100.0% | 41 | 100.0% | 94 | 99.4% | 2,870 |
| Total_length | ±10 percent | 90.0% | 82.9% | 41 | 79.8% | 94 | 90.8% | 2,870 |
| Diameter_age | ±5 years | 95.0% | 41.5% | 41 | 58.5% | 94 | 81.6% | 2,870 |
| Regional Variables | | | | | | | | |
| Site_index_method | No Tolerance | 99.0% | 100.0% | 41 | 100.0% | 94 | 99.8% | 3,003 |
| Field_site_index | No Tolerance | 99.0% | 100.0% | 41 | 100.0% | 94 | 98.3% | 3,003 |
| Results for | | | | 41 SI Trees | | 94 SI Trees | | 3,003 SI Trees |

**Table D.—Observed relative bias values (average [field crew – QA crew]) for measurement variables, blind check plots, 2005**

| Variable | Unit of measure | South Dakota Relative bias | 95% CI limits Lower | 95% CI limits Upper | Number of observations | Plains States Relative bias | 95% CI limits Lower | 95% CI limits Upper | Number of observations | North Central States Relative bias | 95% CI limits Lower | 95% CI limits Upper | Number of observations |
|---|---|---|---|---|---|---|---|---|---|---|---|---|---|
| **Plot Level** | | | | | | | | | | | | | |
| *National Variables* | | | | | | | | | | | | | |
| Distance to Road | code | -0.18 | -0.76 | 0.43 | 34 | -0.15 | -0.42 | 0.13 | 85 | -0.02 | -0.07 | 0.03 | 1,677 |
| *Regional Variables* | | | | | | | | | | | | | |
| ELEVATION_GPS | feet | -42.26 | -111.15 | -4.29 | 31 | -27.20 | -52.73 | -8.78 | 79 | -23.61 | -51.95 | -1.69 | 1,528 |
| LAT_DECIMAL_DEG | degree | 0.00 | 0.00 | 0.00 | 32 | 0.00 | 0.00 | 0.00 | 81 | 0.00 | -0.01 | 0.00 | 1,538 |
| LON_DECIMAL_DEG | degree | 0.00 | 0.00 | 0.00 | 32 | 0.00 | 0.00 | 0.00 | 81 | 0.55 | 0.00 | 1.64 | 1,538 |
| LAT_FEET | feet | 24.87 | -6.64 | 79.44 | 32 | 9.67 | -4.27 | 32.40 | 81 | -1,389.31 | -3,933.65 | -0.09 | 1,538 |
| LON_FEET | feet | -113.32 | -344.86 | 11.68 | 32 | -43.51 | -137.66 | 8.44 | 81 | 8,198.92 | 107.96 | 24,710.51 | 1,538 |
| Results for | | | | | 34 Plots | | | | 85 Plots | | | | 1,677 Plots |
| **Condition Level** | | | | | | | | | | | | | |
| *National Variables* | | | | | | | | | | | | | |
| Stand Size | code | -0.03 | -0.24 | 0.14 | 29 | 0.03 | -0.13 | 0.17 | 75 | 0.01 | -0.01 | 0.02 | 1,810 |
| Stand Age | years | -1.62 | -9.69 | 5.64 | 29 | -1.39 | -4.88 | 1.95 | 75 | -0.72 | -1.28 | -0.24 | 1,810 |
| Results for | | | | | 66 Conditions | | | | 217 Conditions | | | | 2,595 Conditions |
| **Subplot Level** | | | | | | | | | | | | | |
| *National Variables* | | | | | | | | | | | | | |
| Slope | percent | 0.63 | -0.97 | 2.52 | 132 | -0.23 | -1.55 | 0.97 | 328 | 0.63 | 0.16 | 1.21 | 6,535 |
| Aspect | degrees | -6.01 | -20.03 | 6.91 | 116 | -8.36 | -18.23 | -0.41 | 287 | -0.57 | -1.79 | 0.74 | 6,021 |
| Snow/Water Depth | feet | 0.43 | 0.11 | 0.92 | 132 | -0.05 | -0.46 | 0.27 | 328 | -0.40 | -0.55 | -0.25 | 6,535 |
| Results for | | | | | 132 Subplots | | | | 328 Subplots | | | | 6,535 Subplots |
| **Tree Level** | | | | | | | | | | | | | |
| *National Variables* | | | | | | | | | | | | | |
| DBH | inches | -0.12 | -0.24 | -0.01 | 398 | -0.09 | -0.16 | -0.04 | 945 | -0.02 | -0.03 | -0.02 | 27,896 |
| DRC | inches | | | | | 0.11 | -0.15 | 0.43 | 27 | 0.11 | -0.15 | 0.43 | 27 |
| Rotten/Missing Cull | percent | -0.07 | -0.44 | 0.23 | 299 | -0.35 | -0.76 | 0.09 | 813 | 0.02 | -0.04 | 0.07 | 18,782 |
| Total Length | feet | 2.57 | 1.07 | 3.98 | 298 | 1.68 | 0.63 | 2.50 | 789 | 0.30 | 0.08 | 0.52 | 17,997 |
| Actual Length | feet | -2.07 | -8.45 | 3.73 | 35 | -8.82 | -25.30 | 1.11 | 79 | -1.37 | -2.32 | -0.54 | 1,973 |
| Compacted Crown Ratio | percent | -1.70 | -2.80 | -0.54 | 352 | 1.04 | 0.27 | 1.91 | 888 | 0.33 | 0.20 | 0.47 | 24,377 |
| Uncompacted Crown Ratio (P3) | percent | 3.21 | 1.25 | 5.00 | 14 | -27.11 | -34.00 | -19.08 | 75 | -3.32 | -4.29 | -2.26 | 1,061 |

**Continued**

**Table D.—continued**

| Variable | Unit of measure | South Dakota Relative bias | South Dakota 95% CI Lower | South Dakota 95% CI Upper | South Dakota Number of observations | Plains States Relative bias | Plains States 95% CI Lower | Plains States 95% CI Upper | Plains States Number of observations | North Central States Relative bias | North Central States 95% CI Lower | North Central States 95% CI Upper | North Central States Number of observations |
|---|---|---|---|---|---|---|---|---|---|---|---|---|---|
| Crown position | code | 0.07 | 0.00 | 0.21 | 14 | -0.97 | -1.21 | -0.73 | 75 | -0.16 | -0.20 | -0.12 | 850 |
| Crown light exposure | code | -0.29 | -0.64 | 0.18 | 14 | -0.83 | -1.09 | -0.57 | 75 | -0.12 | -0.17 | -0.06 | 1,061 |
| Sapling crown vigor class | code | | | | | | | | | -0.11 | -0.19 | -0.05 | 211 |
| Crown density | percent | -11.07 | -15.00 | -7.50 | 14 | -26.40 | -32.63 | -20.07 | 75 | -3.04 | -4.29 | -2.06 | 850 |
| Crown dieback | percent | 1.43 | 0.36 | 2.50 | 14 | -1.27 | -3.90 | 0.90 | 75 | -0.34 | -0.90 | 0.12 | 850 |
| Transparency | percent | 1.43 | 0.00 | 3.21 | 14 | -15.00 | -18.67 | -11.43 | 75 | -1.76 | -2.61 | -1.06 | 850 |
| Regional Variables | | | | | | | | | | | | | |
| NC Tree Class | code | -0.45 | -0.90 | -0.01 | 397 | 0.12 | -0.16 | 0.34 | 971 | 0.05 | 0.01 | 0.10 | 27,083 |
| DBH-live & decay code 1-2 trees | inches | -0.11 | -0.21 | -0.01 | 370 | -0.09 | -0.15 | -0.03 | 892 | -0.03 | -0.04 | -0.02 | 25,185 |
| DBH-decay code 3-4-5 trees | inches | -0.89 | -1.97 | 0.02 | 11 | -0.31 | -0.70 | -0.04 | 36 | -0.03 | -0.06 | -0.01 | 1,133 |
| Total length trees 40 ft plus | feet | 3.77 | 2.27 | 5.25 | 201 | 2.42 | 1.52 | 3.43 | 459 | 0.75 | 0.60 | 0.87 | 14,813 |
| Total length trees less than 40 ft | feet | 0.07 | -3.88 | 3.65 | 97 | 0.65 | -1.30 | 2.13 | 330 | -1.79 | -2.83 | -0.84 | 3,184 |
| Total Length trees lt 5 inch | feet | | | | | 13.40 | 8.42 | 19.80 | 25 | 2.39 | 0.53 | 4.43 | 230 |
| Results for | | | | | 398 Trees | | | | 972 Trees | | | | 27,923 Trees |
| Seedling Level | | | | | | | | | | | | | |
| National Variables | | | | | | | | | | | | | |
| Seedling Count | number | -2.77 | -21.79 | 15.64 | 42 | -40.39 | -64.46 | -18.12 | 127 | -12.04 | -15.05 | -9.61 | 5,659 |
| Seedling Count coded | number | -0.10 | -0.38 | 0.18 | 42 | -0.34 | -0.56 | -0.10 | 127 | 0.02 | 0.00 | 0.04 | 5,659 |
| Results for | | | | | 32 Microplots | | | | 80 Microplots | | | | 2,402 Microplots |
| Site Tree Level | | | | | | | | | | | | | |
| National Variables | | | | | | | | | | | | | |
| Diameter | inches | -0.28 | -0.68 | -0.05 | 41 | -0.15 | -0.37 | -0.04 | 94 | -0.01 | -0.02 | 0.01 | 2,870 |
| Total_length | feet | -0.63 | -5.06 | 3.63 | 41 | 0.80 | -1.85 | 2.67 | 94 | 0.26 | 0.01 | 0.53 | 2,870 |
| Diameter_age | years | -2.37 | -5.95 | 1.12 | 41 | -1.45 | -3.16 | 0.29 | 94 | 0.15 | -0.05 | 0.34 | 2,870 |
| Regional Variables | | | | | | | | | | | | | |
| Field_site_index | feet | 0.00 | 0.00 | 0.00 | 41 | 0.00 | 0.00 | 0.00 | 94 | 0.09 | 0.01 | 0.19 | 3,003 |
| Results for | | | | | 41 SI Trees | | | | 94 SI Trees | | | | 3,003 SI Trees |

33

Table 1.—Percentage of area by land status, South Dakota, 2005

| Land status | Percentage of area |
|---|---|
| **Accessible forest land** | |
| Unreserved forest land | |
| Timberland | 3.1 |
| Unproductive | 0.2 |
| Total unreserved forest land | 3.3 |
| Reserved forest land | |
| Productive | 0.1 |
| Unproductive | - - |
| Total reserved forest land | 0.1 |
| **All accessible forest land** | 3.4 |
| **Nonforest and other land** | |
| Nonforest land | 93.9 |
| Water | |
| Census | 1.9 |
| Non-Census | 0.6 |
| **All nonforest and other land** | 96.4 |
| **Nonsampled land** | |
| Access denied | 0.2 |
| Hazardous conditions | 0.0 |
| Other | - - |
| **All land** | 100.0 |

| Total area (thousands of acres) | 49,354 |
|---|---|

All table cells without observations in the inventory sample are indicated by --. Table value of 0.0 indicates the percentage rounds to less than 0.1 percent. Columns and rows may not add to their totals due to rounding.

Table 2.—Area of forest land, in thousand acres, by owner class and forest-land status, South Dakota, 2005

| Owner class | Unreserved forests | | | Reserved forests | | | All forest land |
|---|---|---|---|---|---|---|---|
| | Timberland | Unproductive | Total | Productive | Unproductive | Total | |
| **Forest Service** | | | | | | | |
| National forest | 984.0 | 17.6 | 1 001.6 | 31.1 | - - | 31.1 | 1 032.7 |
| **Other Federal** | | | | | | | |
| National Park Service | - - | - - | - - | 17.7 | - - | 17.7 | 17.7 |
| Bureau of Land Management | 39.0 | 5.6 | 44.6 | - - | - - | - - | 44.6 |
| Fish and Wildlife Service | 5.1 | - - | 5.1 | - - | - - | - - | 5.1 |
| Department of Defense or Energy | 5.8 | - - | 5.8 | - - | - - | - - | 5.8 |
| Other Federal | 28.0 | 4.5 | 32.4 | - - | - - | - - | 32.4 |
| **State and local government** | | | | | | | |
| State | 44.3 | 3.3 | 47.6 | 4.4 | - - | 4.4 | 52.0 |
| **Private** | | | | | | | |
| Undifferentiated private | 435.2 | 56.7 | 491.8 | - - | - - | - - | 491.8 |
| **All owners** | 1 541.3 | 87.6 | 1 629.0 | 53.2 | - - | 53.2 | 1 682.1 |

All table cells without observations in the inventory sample are indicated by -- Table value of 0 0 indicates the acres round to less than 0 1 thousand acres Columns and rows may not add to their totals due to rounding

Table 3.—Area of forest land, in thousand acres, by forest-type group and productivity class, South Dakota, 2005

| Forest type group | Site productivity class (cubic feet/acre/year) | | | | | | | All classes |
|---|---|---|---|---|---|---|---|---|
| | 0-19 | 20-49 | 50-84 | 85-119 | 120-164 | 165-224 | 225+ | |
| Spruce / fir group | -- | 32 0 | 24 1 | -- | -- | -- | -- | 56 0 |
| Other eastern softwoods group | 5 8 | 22 2 | -- | -- | -- | -- | -- | 28 0 |
| Pinyon / juniper group | 5 8 | 29 9 | -- | -- | -- | -- | -- | 35 6 |
| Ponderosa pine group | 5 9 | 926 0 | 176 5 | 29 1 | -- | -- | -- | 1 137 5 |
| Oak / hickory group | 45 6 | 76 3 | 10 1 | -- | -- | -- | -- | 131 9 |
| Elm / ash / cottonwood group | 2 2 | 102 8 | -- | 4 3 | -- | -- | -- | 109 3 |
| Maple / beech / birch group | 3 0 | -- | -- | -- | -- | -- | -- | 3 0 |
| Aspen / birch group | 5 9 | 34 6 | 6 3 | -- | 5 1 | -- | -- | 52 0 |
| Other hardwoods group | 3 3 | 10 3 | -- | -- | -- | -- | -- | 13 6 |
| Exotic hardwoods group | -- | 10 8 | -- | -- | -- | -- | -- | 10 8 |
| Nonstocked | 10 2 | 88 3 | 5 8 | -- | -- | -- | -- | 104 3 |
| **All forest type groups** | 87 6 | 1 333 1 | 222 8 | 33 4 | 5 1 | -- | -- | 1 682 1 |

All table cells without observations in the inventory sample are indicated by -- Table value of 0 0 indicates the acres round to less than 0 1 thousand acres Columns and rows may not add to their totals due to rounding

Table 4.—Area of forest land, in thousand acres, by forest-type group, ownership group, and land status, South Dakota, 2005

| Forest type group | Forest Service | | Other Federal | | State and local government | | Undifferentiated private | | All forest land |
| | Timber-land | Other forest land | Timber-land | Other forest land | Timber-land | Other forest land | Timber-land | Other forest land | |
|---|---|---|---|---|---|---|---|---|---|
| Spruce / fir group | 49.9 | -- | 6.1 | -- | -- | -- | -- | -- | 56.0 |
| Other eastern softwoods group | -- | -- | 5.1 | -- | -- | -- | 17.1 | 5.8 | 28.0 |
| Pinyon / juniper group | 5.8 | 5.8 | 16.3 | -- | 1.6 | -- | 6.2 | -- | 35.6 |
| Ponderosa pine group | 807.7 | 37.0 | 25.5 | 17.7 | 38.4 | 4.4 | 206.8 | -- | 1,137.5 |
| Oak / hickory group | 5.0 | -- | 8.9 | 10.1 | -- | -- | 72.4 | 35.5 | 131.9 |
| Elm / ash / cottonwood group | -- | -- | 5.8 | -- | 4.3 | -- | 97.1 | 2.2 | 109.3 |
| Maple / beech / birch group | -- | -- | -- | -- | -- | -- | -- | 3.0 | 3.0 |
| Aspen / birch group | 38.9 | 5.9 | -- | -- | -- | -- | 7.2 | -- | 52.0 |
| Other hardwoods group | 4.3 | -- | 5.9 | -- | -- | 3.3 | -- | -- | 13.6 |
| Exotic hardwoods group | -- | -- | -- | -- | -- | -- | 10.8 | -- | 10.8 |
| Nonstocked | 72.4 | -- | 4.2 | -- | -- | -- | 17.5 | 10.2 | 104.3 |
| **All forest type groups** | 984.0 | 48.7 | 77.8 | 27.8 | 44.3 | 7.7 | 435.2 | 56.7 | 1,682.1 |

All table cells without observations in the inventory sample are indicated by --. Table value of 0.0 indicates the acres round to less than 0.1 thousand acres. Columns and rows may not add to their totals due to rounding.

Table 5.—Area of forest land, in thousand acres, by forest-type group and stand-size class, South Dakota, 2005

| Forest type group | Large diameter | Medium diameter | Stand-size class Small diameter | Chaparral | Nonstocked | All size classes |
|---|---|---|---|---|---|---|
| Spruce / fir group | 42.4 | 6.1 | 7.5 | -- | -- | 56.0 |
| Other eastern softwoods group | 11.3 | 5.8 | 10.9 | -- | -- | 28.0 |
| Pinyon / juniper group | 16.7 | 13.2 | 5.8 | -- | -- | 35.6 |
| Ponderosa pine group | 879.9 | 137.7 | 119.9 | -- | -- | 1 137.5 |
| Oak / hickory group | 43.5 | 69.4 | 19.0 | -- | -- | 131.9 |
| Elm / ash / cottonwood group | 79.5 | 16.5 | 13.4 | -- | -- | 109.3 |
| Maple / beech / birch group | -- | 3.0 | -- | -- | -- | 3.0 |
| Aspen / birch group | 5.8 | 30.8 | 15.5 | -- | -- | 52.0 |
| Other hardwoods group | -- | -- | 13.6 | -- | -- | 13.6 |
| Exotic hardwoods group | -- | 10.8 | -- | -- | -- | 10.8 |
| Nonstocked | -- | -- | -- | -- | 104.3 | 104.3 |
| **All forest type groups** | 1 079.1 | 293.2 | 205.5 | -- | 104.3 | 1 682.1 |

All table cells without observations in the inventory sample are indicated by -- Table value of 0.0 indicates the acres round to less than 0.1 thousand acres Columns and rows may not add to their totals due to rounding

Table 6.—Area of forest land, in thousand acres, by forest-type group and stand-age class, South Dakota, 2005

| Forest type group | Nonstocked | Stand-age (years) | | | | | | All classes |
| | | 0-20 | 21-40 | 41-60 | 61-80 | 81-100 | 100+ | |
|---|---|---|---|---|---|---|---|---|
| Spruce / fir group | -- | 5.2 | -- | 11.7 | 20.5 | 1.0 | 17.6 | 56.0 |
| Other eastern softwoods group | -- | -- | -- | 22.4 | 5.6 | -- | -- | 28.0 |
| Pinyon / juniper group | -- | -- | 10.4 | 11.2 | 6.7 | 5.8 | 1.6 | 35.6 |
| Ponderosa pine group | -- | 23.2 | 66.1 | 135.4 | 354.5 | 335.1 | 223.2 | 1,137.5 |
| Oak / hickory group | -- | -- | 18.5 | 22.6 | 53.6 | 28.3 | 8.8 | 131.9 |
| Elm / ash / cottonwood group | -- | 5.8 | 12.9 | 51.2 | 20.7 | 18.8 | -- | 109.3 |
| Maple / beech / birch group | -- | -- | -- | 3.0 | -- | -- | -- | 3.0 |
| Aspen / birch group | -- | 9.9 | -- | 20.3 | 5.0 | 16.8 | -- | 52.0 |
| Other hardwoods group | -- | 5.9 | 3.3 | -- | -- | 4.3 | -- | 13.6 |
| Exotic hardwoods group | -- | -- | 7.8 | 3.0 | -- | -- | -- | 10.8 |
| Nonstocked | 104.3 | - | - | - | - | - | - | - |
| All forest type groups | - | 50.1 | 119.0 | 280.8 | 466.6 | 410.2 | 251.2 | 1,682.1 |

All table cells without observations in the inventory sample are indicated by --. Table value of 0.0 indicates the acres round to less than 0.1 thousand acres. Columns and rows may not add to their totals due to rounding.

Table 7.—Area of forest land, in thousand acres, by forest-type group and stand origin, South Dakota, 2005

| Forest type group | Stand origin | | All forest land |
|---|---|---|---|
| | Natural stands | Artificial regeneration | |
| Spruce / fir group | 56 0 | - - | 56 0 |
| Other eastern softwoods group | 28 0 | - - | 28 0 |
| Pinyon / juniper group | 35 6 | - - | 35 6 |
| Ponderosa pine group | 1 131 8 | 5 8 | 1 137 5 |
| Oak / hickory group | 126 2 | 5 8 | 131 9 |
| Elm / ash / cottonwood group | 105 5 | 3 8 | 109 3 |
| Maple / beech / birch group | - - | 3 0 | 3 0 |
| Aspen / birch group | 52 0 | - - | 52 0 |
| Other hardwoods group | 13 6 | - - | 13 6 |
| Exotic hardwoods group | 7 8 | 3 0 | 10 8 |
| Nonstocked | 104 3 | - - | 104 3 |
| **All forest type groups** | 1 660 8 | 21 4 | 1 682 1 |

All table cells without observations in the inventory sample are indicated by -- Table value of 0 0 indicates the acres round to less than 0 1 thousand acres Columns and rows may not add to their totals due to rounding

40

Table 8.—Area of forest land, in thousand acres, by forest-type group and primary disturbance class, South Dakota, 2005

| Forest type group | Disturbance class | | | | | | | | | All forest land |
|---|---|---|---|---|---|---|---|---|---|---|
| | None | Insects | Disease | Weather | Fire | Domestic animals | Wild animals | Human | Other | |
| Spruce / fir group | 56 0 | -- | -- | -- | -- | -- | -- | -- | -- | 56 0 |
| Other eastern softwoods group | 22 2 | -- | -- | -- | -- | -- | -- | 5 8 | -- | 28 0 |
| Pinyon / juniper group | 35 6 | -- | -- | -- | -- | -- | -- | -- | -- | 35 6 |
| Ponderosa pine group | 1 050 6 | -- | -- | 27 4 | 36 5 | -- | -- | 23 0 | -- | 1 137 5 |
| Oak / hickory group | 131 9 | -- | -- | -- | -- | -- | -- | -- | -- | 131 9 |
| Elm / ash / cottonwood group | 103 6 | -- | -- | 5 8 | -- | -- | -- | -- | -- | 109 3 |
| Maple / beech / birch group | 3 0 | -- | -- | -- | -- | -- | -- | -- | -- | 3 0 |
| Aspen / birch group | 40 4 | -- | -- | -- | 11 7 | -- | -- | -- | -- | 52 0 |
| Other hardwoods group | 13 6 | -- | -- | -- | -- | -- | -- | -- | -- | 13 6 |
| Exotic hardwoods group | 10 8 | -- | -- | -- | -- | -- | -- | -- | -- | 10 8 |
| Nonstocked | 30 0 | -- | -- | 5 1 | 69 2 | -- | -- | -- | -- | 104 3 |
| **All forest type groups** | **1 497 7** | -- | -- | **38 2** | **117 4** | -- | -- | **28 8** | -- | **1 682 1** |

All table cells without observations in the inventory sample are indicated by -- Table value of 0 0 indicates the acres round to less than 0 1 thousand acres  Columns and rows may not add to their totals due to rounding

41

Table 9.—Area of timberland, in thousand acres, by forest-type group and stand-size class, South Dakota, 2005

| Forest type group | Large diameter | Medium diameter | Stand-size class<br>Small diameter | Chaparral | Nonstocked | All size classes |
|---|---|---|---|---|---|---|
| Spruce / fir group | 42 4 | 6 1 | 7 5 | -- | -- | 56 0 |
| Other eastern softwoods group | 11 3 | 5 8 | 5 1 | -- | -- | 22 2 |
| Pinyon / juniper group | 10 9 | 13 2 | 5 8 | -- | -- | 29 9 |
| Ponderosa pine group | 832 5 | 134 9 | 111 0 | -- | -- | 1 078 4 |
| Oak / hickory group | 30 9 | 36 4 | 19 0 | -- | -- | 86 4 |
| Elm / ash / cottonwood group | 79 5 | 14 3 | 13 4 | -- | -- | 107 2 |
| Aspen / birch group | 5 8 | 24 8 | 15 5 | -- | -- | 46 1 |
| Other hardwoods group | -- | -- | 10 3 | -- | -- | 10 3 |
| Exotic hardwoods group | -- | 10 8 | -- | -- | -- | 10 8 |
| Nonstocked | -- | -- | -- | -- | 94 1 | 94 1 |
| **All forest type groups** | 1 013 3 | 246 4 | 187 6 | -- | 94 1 | 1 541 3 |

All table cells without observations in the inventory sample are indicated by -- Table value of 0 0 indicates the acres round to less than 0 1 thousand acres Columns and rows may not add to their totals due to rounding

Table 10.—Number of live trees, in thousands, on forest land by species group and diameter class, South Dakota, 2005

| Species group | Diameter class (inches) | | | | | | | | | | | | | | | All classes |
|---|---|---|---|---|---|---|---|---|---|---|---|---|---|---|---|---|
| | 1.0-2.9 | 3.0-4.9 | 5.0-6.9 | 7.0-8.9 | 9.0-10.9 | 11.0-12.9 | 13.0-14.9 | 15.0-16.9 | 17.0-18.9 | 19.0-20.9 | 21.0-24.9 | 25.0-28.9 | 29.0-32.9 | 33.0-36.9 | 37.0+ | |
| Softwood species groups | | | | | | | | | | | | | | | | |
| Eastern softwood species groups | | | | | | | | | | | | | | | | |
| Spruce and balsam fir | 11,362 | 5,726 | 2,173 | 2,216 | 1,751 | 898 | 972 | 522 | 136 | 108 | -- | -- | -- | -- | -- | 25,864 |
| Other eastern softwoods | 132,388 | 55,024 | 43,738 | 44,335 | 31,078 | 18,385 | 10,738 | 6,061 | 3,617 | 1,633 | 800 | 220 | 63 | -- | -- | 346,081 |
| All softwoods | 143,750 | 60,750 | 45,911 | 46,551 | 32,829 | 19,283 | 11,710 | 6,583 | 3,754 | 1,741 | 800 | 220 | 63 | -- | -- | 373,945 |
| Hardwood species groups | | | | | | | | | | | | | | | | |
| Eastern hardwood species groups | | | | | | | | | | | | | | | | |
| Select white oaks | 2,627 | 11,399 | 6,662 | 4,196 | 1,652 | 1,101 | 605 | 312 | 234 | 72 | 105 | -- | -- | -- | -- | 29,162 |
| Hard maple | -- | -- | -- | -- | 26 | 26 | -- | -- | -- | -- | -- | -- | -- | -- | -- | 52 |
| Soft maple | -- | -- | 36 | 108 | 108 | 36 | 36 | -- | -- | -- | -- | -- | -- | -- | -- | 325 |
| Ash | 8,224 | 1,810 | 3,021 | 2,185 | 1,534 | 683 | 436 | 269 | 72 | 208 | 100 | 39 | -- | -- | -- | 18,581 |
| Cottonwood and aspen | 15,933 | 2,616 | 3,932 | 2,365 | 788 | 212 | 271 | 164 | 110 | 118 | 88 | 105 | 70 | -- | 36 | 26,809 |
| Basswood | -- | 432 | 130 | 26 | 31 | -- | -- | -- | -- | -- | -- | -- | -- | -- | -- | 618 |
| Other eastern soft hardwoods | 14,136 | 5,745 | 3,593 | 2,175 | 1,272 | 708 | 321 | 238 | 180 | 108 | 110 | 71 | -- | -- | -- | 28,657 |
| Other eastern hard hardwoods | -- | -- | 78 | -- | 26 | -- | -- | -- | -- | -- | -- | -- | -- | -- | -- | 105 |
| Eastern noncommercial hardwoods | 26,714 | 5,510 | 808 | 166 | 76 | -- | -- | -- | -- | -- | -- | -- | -- | -- | -- | 33,274 |
| All hardwoods | 67,633 | 27,512 | 18,460 | 11,221 | 5,513 | 2,766 | 1,669 | 983 | 597 | 506 | 403 | 215 | 70 | -- | 36 | 137,583 |
| All species groups | 211,382 | 88,263 | 64,371 | 57,772 | 36,342 | 22,049 | 13,379 | 7,566 | 4,350 | 2,247 | 1,203 | 435 | 134 | -- | 36 | 511,529 |

All table cells without observations in the inventory sample are indicated by --. Table value of 0 indicates the number of trees rounds to less than 1 thousand trees. Columns and rows may not add to their totals due to rounding.

Table 11.—Number of growing-stock trees, in thousands, on timberland by species group and diameter class, South Dakota, 2005

| Species group | Diameter class (inches) | | | | | | | | | | | | | All classes |
|---|---|---|---|---|---|---|---|---|---|---|---|---|---|---|
| | 5.0-6.9 | 7.0-8.9 | 9.0-10.9 | 11.0-12.9 | 13.0-14.9 | 15.0-16.9 | 17.0-18.9 | 19.0-20.9 | 21.0-24.9 | 25.0-28.9 | 29.0-32.9 | 33.0-36.9 | 37.0+ | |
| **Softwood species groups** | | | | | | | | | | | | | | |
| **Eastern softwood species groups** | | | | | | | | | | | | | | |
| Spruce and balsam fir | 2,173 | 2,179 | 1,751 | 898 | 937 | 522 | 136 | 108 | -- | -- | -- | -- | -- | 8,705 |
| Other eastern softwoods | 38,590 | 40,960 | 28,726 | 17,089 | 10,212 | 5,506 | 3,226 | 1,465 | 589 | 220 | 63 | -- | -- | 146,647 |
| **All softwoods** | 40,763 | 43,139 | 30,477 | 17,987 | 11,149 | 6,028 | 3,363 | 1,573 | 589 | 220 | 63 | -- | -- | 155,351 |
| **Hardwood species groups** | | | | | | | | | | | | | | |
| **Eastern hardwood species groups** | | | | | | | | | | | | | | |
| Select white oaks | 3,800 | 2,059 | 660 | 413 | 194 | 106 | 89 | 36 | 69 | -- | -- | -- | -- | 7,426 |
| Hard maple | -- | -- | 26 | 26 | -- | -- | -- | -- | -- | -- | -- | -- | -- | 52 |
| Soft maple | -- | 36 | 72 | -- | -- | -- | -- | -- | -- | -- | -- | -- | -- | 108 |
| Ash | 1,972 | 1,387 | 1,028 | 405 | 272 | 137 | 36 | -- | 35 | 39 | -- | -- | -- | 5,310 |
| Cottonwood and aspen | 3,149 | 1,907 | 611 | 177 | 235 | 164 | 110 | 118 | 88 | 105 | 70 | -- | 36 | 6,772 |
| Basswood | 130 | 26 | 31 | -- | -- | -- | -- | -- | -- | -- | -- | -- | -- | 187 |
| Other eastern soft hardwoods | 2,392 | 1,401 | 622 | 144 | 70 | 71 | 36 | 36 | -- | 36 | -- | -- | -- | 4,808 |
| Other eastern hard hardwoods | 26 | -- | -- | -- | -- | -- | -- | -- | -- | -- | -- | -- | -- | 26 |
| **All hardwoods** | 11,469 | 6,817 | 3,050 | 1,165 | 772 | 477 | 272 | 190 | 192 | 180 | 70 | -- | 36 | 24,690 |
| **All species groups** | 52,232 | 49,956 | 33,527 | 19,152 | 11,921 | 6,505 | 3,634 | 1,764 | 781 | 400 | 134 | -- | 36 | 180,041 |

All table cells without observations in the inventory sample are indicated by --. Table value of 0 indicates the number of trees rounds to less than 1 thousand trees. Columns and rows may not add to their totals due to rounding.

Table 12.—Net volume of all live trees, in million cubic feet, by owner class and forest-land status, South Dakota, 2005

| Owner class | Unreserved forests | | | Reserved forests | | | All forest land |
|---|---|---|---|---|---|---|---|
| | Timberland | Unproductive | Total | Productive | Unproductive | Total | |
| Forest Service | | | | | | | |
| National forest | 1 383 7 | 9 7 | 1 393 4 | 65 7 | - - | 65 7 | 1 459 2 |
| Other Federal | | | | | | | |
| National Park Service | - - | - - | - - | 16 7 | - - | 16 7 | 16 7 |
| Bureau of Land Management | 49 9 | 1 2 | 51 0 | - - | - - | - - | 51 0 |
| Fish and Wildlife Service | 0 8 | - - | 0 8 | - - | - - | - - | 0 8 |
| Other Federal | 20 4 | 6 0 | 26 4 | - - | - - | - - | 26 4 |
| State and local government | | | | | | | |
| State | 82 3 | 0 2 | 82 4 | 2 5 | - - | 2 5 | 84 9 |
| Private | | | | | | | |
| Undifferentiated private | 484 4 | 43 1 | 527 5 | - - | - - | - - | 527 5 |
| All owners | 2 021 5 | 60 1 | 2 081 6 | 84 9 | - - | 84 9 | 2 166 5 |

All table cells without observations in the inventory sample are indicated by -- Table value of 0 0 indicates the volume rounds to less than 0 1 million cubic feet Columns and rows may not add to their totals due to rounding

45

Table 13.—Net volume of all live trees, in million cubic feet, on forest land by forest-type group and stand-size class, South Dakota, 2005

| Forest type group | Stand-size class | | | | | All size classes |
| | Large diameter | Medium diameter | Small diameter | Chaparral | Nonstocked | |
| --- | --- | --- | --- | --- | --- | --- |
| Spruce / fir group | 71 4 | 7 8 | 3 0 | - - | - - | 82 2 |
| Other eastern softwoods group | 4 2 | 1 3 | 2 2 | - - | - - | 7 7 |
| Pinyon / juniper group | 19 6 | 5 5 | 2 4 | - - | - - | 27 5 |
| Ponderosa pine group | 1 485 4 | 149 1 | 56 8 | - - | - - | 1 691 3 |
| Oak / hickory group | 89 1 | 59 1 | 7 4 | - - | - - | 155 5 |
| Elm / ash / cottonwood group | 143 6 | 18 6 | 1 4 | - - | - - | 163 6 |
| Maple / beech / birch group | - - | 1 2 | - - | - - | - - | 1 2 |
| Aspen / birch group | 3 8 | 18 0 | 3 5 | - - | - - | 25 3 |
| Other hardwoods group | - - | - - | 1 7 | - - | - - | 1 7 |
| Exotic hardwoods group | - - | 5 4 | - - | - - | - - | 5 4 |
| Nonstocked | - - | - - | - - | - - | 5 0 | 5 0 |
| **All forest type groups** | 1 817 2 | 265 9 | 78 5 | - - | 5 0 | 2 166 5 |

All table cells without observations in the inventory sample are indicated by -- Table value of 0 0 indicates the volume rounds to less than 0 1 million cubic feet  Columns and rows may not add to their totals due to rounding

Table 13a.—Net volume of all live trees, in million cubic feet, on forest land by species and forest-type group. South Dakota, 2005

| Species | Spruce/fir | Other eastern softwoods | Pinyon/juniper | Ponderosa pine | Oak/hickory | Elm/ash/cottonwood | Maple/beech/birch | Aspen/birch | Other hardwoods | Exotic hardwoods | Nonstocked | All forest type groups |
|---|---|---|---|---|---|---|---|---|---|---|---|---|
| American basswood | - | - | - | - | 0.6 | - | - | - | - | - | - | 0.6 |
| American elm | - | 0.3 | - | 0.2 | 7.6 | 25.4 | 1.2 | - | 0.2 | 1.1 | - | 36.0 |
| boxelder | - | - | - | - | 3.1 | 22.4 | - | - | - | - | 0.4 | 25.9 |
| bur oak | - | 0.9 | - | 6.9 | 82.8 | 6.4 | - | - | - | - | - | 97.0 |
| chokecherry | - | - | - | - | - | 0.0 | - | - | - | - | - | 0.0 |
| eastern cottonwood | - | - | - | - | - | 68.1 | - | - | - | - | - | 68.1 |
| eastern hophornbeam | - | 0.0 | - | - | 1.3 | - | - | - | - | - | - | 1.4 |
| eastern redcedar | - | 6.1 | - | 0.0 | 1.5 | 0.1 | - | - | - | - | - | 7.8 |
| green ash | - | 0.4 | - | 0.3 | 40.0 | 29.9 | - | - | - | 0.3 | 1.4 | 72.2 |
| hackberry | - | - | - | - | - | 3.2 | - | - | - | - | - | 3.2 |
| paper birch | 0.3 | - | - | 1.1 | 0.1 | - | - | 0.9 | 0.0 | - | - | 2.4 |
| ponderosa pine | 26.2 | - | 7.4 | 1 639.8 | 17.6 | - | - | 10.8 | 1.5 | - | 3.2 | 1 706.5 |
| prairie crab apple | - | - | - | - | 0.1 | - | - | - | - | - | - | 0.1 |
| quaking aspen | 3.4 | - | - | 8.6 | - | - | - | 13.6 | - | - | - | 25.6 |
| red mulberry | - | - | - | - | - | 0.3 | - | - | - | - | - | 0.3 |
| Rocky Mountain juniper | - | - | 20.1 | 4.5 | - | - | - | - | - | - | - | 24.6 |
| Siberian elm | - | - | - | - | - | - | - | - | - | 4.0 | - | 4.0 |
| silver maple | - | - | - | - | - | 3.1 | - | - | - | - | - | 3.1 |
| sugar maple | - | - | - | - | 0.8 | - | - | - | - | - | - | 0.8 |
| white spruce | 52.3 | - | - | 29.9 | - | - | - | - | - | - | - | 82.2 |
| white willow | - | - | - | - | - | 3.9 | - | - | - | - | - | 3.9 |
| willow spp | - | - | - | - | - | 0.8 | - | - | - | - | - | 0.8 |
| All species | 82.2 | 7.7 | 27.5 | 1 691.3 | 155.5 | 163.6 | 1.2 | 25.3 | 1.7 | 5.4 | 5.0 | 2 166.5 |

47

Table 14.—Net volume of all live trees, in million cubic feet, on forest land by species group and ownership group, South Dakota, 2005

| | Ownership group | | | | |
| Species group | Forest Service | Other Federal | State and local government | Undifferentiated private | All owners |
|---|---|---|---|---|---|
| **Softwood species groups** | | | | | |
| **Eastern softwood species groups** | | | | | |
| Spruce and balsam fir | 73.0 | 7.2 | -- | 2.1 | 82.2 |
| Other eastern softwoods | 1,357.0 | 69.4 | 71.8 | 240.6 | 1,738.8 |
| **All softwoods** | 1,430.0 | 76.6 | 71.8 | 242.6 | 1,821.0 |
| **Hardwood species groups** | | | | | |
| **Eastern hardwood species groups** | | | | | |
| Select white oaks | 4.4 | 13.7 | -- | 79.0 | 97.0 |
| Hard maple | -- | -- | -- | 0.8 | 0.8 |
| Soft maple | -- | -- | -- | 3.1 | 3.1 |
| Ash | 0.3 | 1.4 | -- | 70.5 | 72.2 |
| Cottonwood and aspen | 22.1 | 1.3 | 11.9 | 58.4 | 93.6 |
| Basswood | -- | -- | -- | 0.6 | 0.6 |
| Other eastern soft hardwoods | 2.1 | 1.9 | 1.0 | 70.5 | 75.4 |
| Other eastern hard hardwoods | -- | -- | 0.3 | -- | 0.3 |
| Eastern noncommercial hardwoods | 0.3 | -- | -- | 2.1 | 2.3 |
| **All hardwoods** | 29.1 | 18.3 | 13.2 | 284.9 | 345.5 |
| **All species groups** | 1,459.2 | 94.9 | 84.9 | 527.5 | 2,166.5 |

All table cells without observations in the inventory sample are indicated by -- Table value of 0 0 indicates the volume rounds to less than 0 1 million cubic feet Columns and rows may not add to their totals due to rounding

Table 15.—Net volume of all live trees, in million cubic feet, on forest land by species group and diameter class, South Dakota, 2005

| Species group | Diameter class (inches) | | | | | | | | | | | | | All classes |
|---|---|---|---|---|---|---|---|---|---|---|---|---|---|---|
| | 5.0-6.9 | 7.0-8.9 | 9.0-10.9 | 11.0-12.9 | 13.0-14.9 | 15.0-16.9 | 17.0-18.9 | 19.0-20.9 | 21.0-24.9 | 25.0-28.9 | 29.0-32.9 | 33.0-36.9 | 37.0+ | |
| Softwood species groups | | | | | | | | | | | | | | |
| Eastern softwood species groups | | | | | | | | | | | | | | |
| Spruce and balsam fir | 5 | 10 | 14 | 11 | 18 | 14 | 5 | 5 | -- | -- | -- | -- | -- | 82 |
| Other eastern softwoods | 77 | 217 | 305 | 292 | 262 | 210 | 167 | 100 | 70 | 32 | 8 | -- | -- | 1,739 |
| All softwoods | 81 | 227 | 319 | 303 | 280 | 224 | 172 | 105 | 70 | 32 | 8 | -- | -- | 1,821 |
| Hardwood species groups | | | | | | | | | | | | | | |
| Eastern hardwood species groups | | | | | | | | | | | | | | |
| Select white oaks | 14 | 18 | 13 | 14 | 11 | 8 | 8 | 3 | 7 | -- | -- | -- | -- | 97 |
| Hard maple | -- | -- | 0 | 0 | -- | -- | -- | -- | -- | -- | -- | -- | -- | 1 |
| Soft maple | 0 | 1 | 1 | 1 | 1 | -- | -- | -- | -- | -- | -- | -- | -- | 3 |
| Ash | 6 | 9 | 12 | 8 | 9 | 7 | 3 | 7 | 7 | 4 | -- | -- | -- | 72 |
| Cottonwood and aspen | 9 | 11 | 7 | 3 | 6 | 5 | 5 | 7 | 6 | 13 | 11 | -- | 11 | 94 |
| Basswood | 0 | 0 | 0 | -- | -- | -- | -- | -- | -- | -- | -- | -- | -- | 1 |
| Other eastern soft hardwoods | 7 | 9 | 10 | 9 | 6 | 6 | 7 | 6 | 8 | 8 | -- | -- | -- | 75 |
| Other eastern hard hardwoods | 0 | -- | 0 | -- | -- | -- | -- | -- | -- | -- | -- | -- | -- | 0 |
| Eastern noncommercial hardwoods | 1 | 1 | 0 | -- | -- | -- | -- | -- | -- | -- | -- | -- | -- | 2 |
| All hardwoods | 38 | 49 | 44 | 36 | 33 | 27 | 22 | 23 | 27 | 24 | 11 | -- | 11 | 345 |
| All species groups | 120 | 276 | 363 | 339 | 313 | 251 | 194 | 128 | 97 | 56 | 19 | -- | 11 | 2,166 |

All table cells without observations in the inventory sample are indicated by --. Table value of 0 indicates the volume rounds to less than 1 million cubic feet. Columns and rows may not add to their totals due to rounding.

Table 16.—Net volume of all live trees, in million cubic feet, on forest land by forest-type group and stand origin, South Dakota, 2005

| Forest type group | Stand origin | | All forest land |
|---|---|---|---|
| | Natural stands | Artificial regeneration | |
| Spruce / fir group | 82 2 | - - | 82 2 |
| Other eastern softwoods group | 7 7 | - - | 7 7 |
| Pinyon / juniper group | 27 5 | - - | 27 5 |
| Ponderosa pine group | 1 686 9 | 4 4 | 1 691 3 |
| Oak / hickory group | 148 7 | 6 9 | 155 5 |
| Elm / ash / cottonwood group | 153 6 | 10 0 | 163 6 |
| Maple / beech / birch group | - - | 1 2 | 1 2 |
| Aspen / birch group | 25 3 | - - | 25 3 |
| Other hardwoods group | 1 7 | - - | 1 7 |
| Exotic hardwoods group | 3 9 | 1 5 | 5 4 |
| Nonstocked | 5 0 | - - | 5 0 |
| **All forest type groups** | **2 142 5** | **24 0** | **2 166 5** |

All table cells without observations in the inventory sample are indicated by -- Table value of 0 0 indicates the volume rounds to less than 0 1 million cubic feet  Columns and rows may not add to their totals due to rounding

Table 17.—Net volume of growing-stock trees, in million cubic feet, on timberland by species group and diameter class, South Dakota , 2005

| Species group | Diameter class (inches) | | | | | | | | | | | | | All classes |
|---|---|---|---|---|---|---|---|---|---|---|---|---|---|---|
| | 5.0-6.9 | 7.0-8.9 | 9.0-10.9 | 11.0-12.9 | 13.0-14.9 | 15.0-16.9 | 17.0-18.9 | 19.0-20.9 | 21.0-24.9 | 25.0-28.9 | 29.0-32.9 | 33.0-36.9 | 37.0+ | |
| **Softwood species groups** | | | | | | | | | | | | | | |
| Eastern softwood species groups | | | | | | | | | | | | | | |
| Spruce and balsam fir | 5 | 9 | 14 | 11 | 18 | 14 | 5 | 5 | -- | -- | -- | -- | -- | 81 |
| Other eastern softwoods | 69 | 204 | 286 | 275 | 251 | 193 | 150 | 89 | 54 | 32 | 8 | -- | -- | 1,612 |
| **All softwoods** | 74 | 213 | 300 | 286 | 269 | 207 | 155 | 94 | 54 | 32 | 8 | -- | -- | 1,693 |
| **Hardwood species groups** | | | | | | | | | | | | | | |
| Eastern hardwood species groups | | | | | | | | | | | | | | |
| Select white oaks | 8 | 9 | 5 | 6 | 4 | 3 | 3 | 2 | 4 | -- | -- | -- | -- | 45 |
| Hard maple | -- | -- | 0 | 0 | -- | -- | -- | -- | -- | -- | -- | -- | -- | 1 |
| Soft maple | -- | 0 | 1 | -- | -- | -- | -- | -- | -- | -- | -- | -- | -- | 1 |
| Ash | 4 | 6 | 9 | 5 | 6 | 4 | 1 | -- | 3 | 4 | -- | -- | -- | 42 |
| Cottonwood and aspen | 7 | 9 | 5 | 2 | 5 | 5 | 5 | 7 | 6 | 13 | 11 | -- | 11 | 88 |
| Basswood | 0 | 0 | 0 | -- | -- | -- | -- | -- | -- | -- | -- | -- | -- | 1 |
| Other eastern soft hardwoods | 5 | 6 | 5 | 2 | 1 | 2 | 1 | 2 | -- | 4 | -- | -- | -- | 28 |
| Other eastern hard hardwoods | 0 | -- | -- | -- | -- | -- | -- | -- | -- | -- | -- | -- | -- | 0 |
| **All hardwoods** | 24 | 31 | 26 | 16 | 16 | 14 | 11 | 11 | 13 | 20 | 11 | -- | 11 | 205 |
| **All species groups** | 98 | 245 | 326 | 302 | 285 | 221 | 166 | 105 | 67 | 52 | 19 | -- | 11 | 1,898 |

All table cells without observations in the inventory sample are indicated by --. Table value of 0 indicates the volume rounds to less than 1 million cubic feet. Columns and rows may not add to their totals due to rounding.

Table 18.—Net volume of growing-stock trees, in million cubic feet, on timberland by species group and ownership group, South Dakota, 2005

| Species group | Ownership group | | | | |
|---|---|---|---|---|---|
| | Forest Service | Other Federal | State and local government | Undifferentiated private | All owners |
| **Softwood species groups** | | | | | |
| Eastern softwood species groups | | | | | |
| Spruce and balsam fir | 72.0 | 7.2 | -- | 2.1 | 81.3 |
| Other eastern softwoods | 1 276.3 | 34.6 | 68.3 | 232.8 | 1 612.0 |
| **All softwoods** | 1 348.3 | 41.8 | 68.3 | 234.9 | 1 693.3 |
| **Hardwood species groups** | | | | | |
| Eastern hardwood species groups | | | | | |
| Select white oaks | 4.4 | 5.8 | -- | 34.4 | 44.6 |
| Hard maple | -- | -- | -- | 0.8 | 0.8 |
| Soft maple | -- | -- | -- | 0.9 | 0.9 |
| Ash | 0.2 | 0.2 | -- | 41.6 | 42.0 |
| Cottonwood and aspen | 18.0 | 1.3 | 11.9 | 56.6 | 87.8 |
| Basswood | -- | -- | -- | 0.6 | 0.6 |
| Other eastern soft hardwoods | 1.7 | 1.9 | 0.4 | 24.2 | 28.2 |
| Other eastern hard hardwoods | -- | -- | 0.1 | -- | 0.1 |
| **All hardwoods** | 24.3 | 9.2 | 12.3 | 159.1 | 204.9 |
| **All species groups** | 1 372.7 | 50.9 | 80.6 | 394.0 | 1 898.2 |

All table cells without observations in the inventory sample are indicated by -- Table value of 0 0 indicates the volume rounds to less than 0 1 million cubic feet Columns and rows may not add to their totals due to rounding

Table 19.—Net volume of sawtimber trees, in million board feet, (International 1/4-inch rule) on timberland by species group and diameter class, South Dakota, 2005

| Species group | Diameter class (inches) | | | | | | | | | | | All classes |
|---|---|---|---|---|---|---|---|---|---|---|---|---|
| | 9.0-10.9 | 11.0-12.9 | 13.0-14.9 | 15.0-16.9 | 17.0-18.9 | 19.0-20.9 | 21.0-24.9 | 25.0-28.9 | 29.0-32.9 | 33.0-36.9 | 37.0+ | |
| Softwood species groups | | | | | | | | | | | | |
| Eastern softwood species groups | | | | | | | | | | | | |
| Spruce and balsam fir | 59 | 48 | 74 | 58 | 21 | 23 | -- | -- | -- | -- | -- | 283 |
| Other eastern softwoods | 733 | 1,056 | 1,130 | 959 | 794 | 491 | 309 | 192 | 45 | -- | -- | 5,708 |
| All softwoods | 792 | 1,103 | 1,204 | 1,017 | 815 | 514 | 309 | 192 | 45 | -- | -- | 5,991 |
| Hardwood species groups | | | | | | | | | | | | |
| Eastern hardwood species groups | | | | | | | | | | | | |
| Select white oaks | -- | 28 | 17 | 15 | 15 | 10 | 22 | -- | -- | -- | -- | 107 |
| Hard maple | -- | 2 | -- | -- | -- | -- | -- | -- | -- | -- | -- | 2 |
| Ash | -- | 22 | 25 | 17 | 7 | -- | 13 | 18 | -- | -- | -- | 102 |
| Cottonwood and aspen | -- | 11 | 24 | 25 | 24 | 35 | 33 | 65 | 55 | -- | 51 | 322 |
| Other eastern soft hardwoods | -- | 8 | 6 | 9 | 6 | 9 | -- | 19 | -- | -- | -- | 56 |
| All hardwoods | -- | 72 | 73 | 65 | 51 | 54 | 68 | 102 | 55 | -- | 51 | 589 |
| All species groups | 792 | 1,175 | 1,276 | 1,082 | 866 | 568 | 377 | 294 | 100 | -- | 51 | 6,580 |

All table cells without observations in the inventory sample are indicated by --. Table value of 0 indicates the volume rounds to less than 1 million board feet. Columns and rows may not add to their totals due to rounding.

Table 19a.—Net volume of sawtimber trees, in million board feet, (Doyle rule) on timberland by species group and diameter class, South Dakota, 2005

| Species group | Diameter class (inches) | | | | | | | | | | | All classes |
| --- | --- | --- | --- | --- | --- | --- | --- | --- | --- | --- | --- | --- |
| | 9.0-10.9 | 11.0-12.9 | 13.0-14.9 | 15.0-16.9 | 17.0-18.9 | 19.0-20.9 | 21.0-24.9 | 25.0-28.9 | 29.0-32.9 | 33.0-36.9 | 37.0+ | |
| Softwood species groups | | | | | | | | | | | | |
| Eastern softwood species groups | | | | | | | | | | | | |
| Spruce and balsam fir | 20 | 23 | 44 | 40 | 16 | 20 | - - | - - | - - | - - | - - | 164 |
| Other eastern softwoods | 253 | 505 | 677 | 662 | 610 | 421 | 277 | 183 | 50 | - - | - - | 3,638 |
| All softwoods | 274 | 527 | 721 | 702 | 626 | 441 | 277 | 183 | 50 | - - | - - | 3,801 |
| Hardwood species groups | | | | | | | | | | | | |
| Eastern hardwood species groups | | | | | | | | | | | | |
| Select white oaks | - - | 12 | 9 | 9 | 10 | 7 | 18 | - - | - - | - - | - - | 64 |
| Hard maple | - - | 1 | - - | - - | - - | - - | - - | - - | - - | - - | - - | 1 |
| Ash | - - | 9 | 13 | 10 | 4 | - - | 10 | 16 | - - | - - | - - | 62 |
| Cottonwood and aspen | - - | 4 | 12 | 15 | 15 | 25 | 26 | 58 | 62 | - - | 58 | 276 |
| Other eastern soft hardwoods | - - | 3 | 3 | 5 | 4 | 6 | - - | 18 | - - | - - | - - | 40 |
| All hardwoods | - - | 30 | 37 | 38 | 33 | 39 | 54 | 92 | 62 | - - | 58 | 443 |
| All species groups | 274 | 557 | 758 | 741 | 660 | 479 | 331 | 274 | 113 | - - | 58 | 4,245 |

All table cells without observations in the inventory sample are indicated by --. Table value of 0 indicates the volume rounds to less than 1 million board feet. Columns and rows may not add to their totals due to rounding.

Table 20.—Net volume of saw-log portion of sawtimber trees, in million cubic feet, on timberland by species group and ownership group, South Dakota, 2005

| Species group | Ownership group | | | | |
| --- | --- | --- | --- | --- | --- |
| | Forest Service | Other Federal | State and local government | Undifferentiated private | All owners |
| **Softwood species groups** | | | | | |
| Eastern softwood species groups | | | | | |
| Spruce and balsam fir | 52 8 | 4 6 | - - | 1 6 | 59 0 |
| Other eastern softwoods | 881 6 | 26 9 | 57 6 | 171 3 | 1 137 4 |
| **All softwoods** | 934 4 | 31 5 | 57 6 | 172 9 | 1 196 4 |
| **Hardwood species groups** | | | | | |
| Eastern hardwood species groups | | | | | |
| Select white oaks | 0 8 | 3 8 | - - | 14 0 | 18 6 |
| Hard maple | - - | - - | - - | 0 4 | 0 4 |
| Ash | - - | - - | - - | 18 5 | 18 5 |
| Cottonwood and aspen | 1 0 | 0 5 | 11 0 | 49 7 | 62 2 |
| Other eastern soft hardwoods | - - | 0 6 | - - | 10 0 | 10 6 |
| **All hardwoods** | 1 8 | 4 9 | 11 0 | 92 7 | 110 4 |
| **All species groups** | 936 2 | 36 4 | 68 6 | 265 6 | 1 306 8 |

All table cells without observations in the inventory sample are indicated by -- Table value of 0 0 indicates the volume rounds to less than 0 1 million cubic feet Columns and rows may not add to their totals due to rounding

Table 31.—Live-tree aboveground dry weight, in thousand dry tons, (CRM) by owner class and forest-land status, South Dakota, 2005

| Owner class | Unreserved forests | | | Reserved forests | | | All forest land |
|---|---|---|---|---|---|---|---|
| | Timberland | Unproductive | Total | Productive | Unproductive | Total | |
| **Forest Service** | | | | | | | |
| National forest | 26 023 | 172 | 26 195 | 1 220 | - - | 1 220 | 27 415 |
| **Other Federal** | | | | | | | |
| National Park Service | - - | - - | - - | 323 | - - | 323 | 323 |
| Bureau of Land Management | 898 | 34 | 932 | - - | - - | - - | 932 |
| Fish and Wildlife Service | 22 | - - | 22 | - - | - - | - - | 22 |
| Department of Defense or Energy | 0 | - - | 0 | - - | - - | - - | 0 |
| Other Federal | 463 | 169 | 632 | - - | - - | - - | 632 |
| **State and local government** | | | | | | | |
| State | 1 497 | 5 | 1 501 | 44 | - - | 44 | 1 545 |
| **Private** | | | | | | | |
| Undifferentiated private | 10 604 | 1 233 | 11 837 | - - | - - | - - | 11 837 |
| **All owners** | 39 508 | 1 612 | 41 120 | 1 587 | - - | 1 587 | 42 706 |

All table cells without observations in the inventory sample are indicated by -- Table value of 0 indicates the aboveground tree biomass rounds to less than 1 thousand dry tons Columns and rows may not add to their totals due to rounding

Table 32.—Live-tree aboveground dry weight, in thousand dry tons, (CRM) on forest land by species group and diameter class, South Dakota, 2005

| Species group | Diameter class (inches) | | | | | | | | | | | | | | | All classes |
|---|---|---|---|---|---|---|---|---|---|---|---|---|---|---|---|---|
| | 1.0-2.9 | 3.0-4.9 | 5.0-6.9 | 7.0-8.9 | 9.0-10.9 | 11.0-12.9 | 13.0-14.9 | 15.0-16.9 | 17.0-18.9 | 19.0-20.9 | 21.0-22.9 | 23.0-24.9 | 25.0-26.9 | 27.0-28.9 | 29.0+ | |
| **Softwood species groups** | | | | | | | | | | | | | | | | |
| Eastern softwood species groups | | | | | | | | | | | | | | | | |
| Spruce and balsam fir | 34 | 84 | 81 | 160 | 231 | 183 | 295 | 220 | 79 | 86 | -- | -- | -- | -- | -- | 1,453 |
| Other eastern softwoods | 212 | 533 | 1,436 | 3,988 | 5,551 | 5,267 | 4,703 | 3,752 | 2,968 | 1,768 | 615 | 604 | 569 | -- | 136 | 32,102 |
| **All softwoods** | 246 | 617 | 1,518 | 4,148 | 5,782 | 5,450 | 4,998 | 3,972 | 3,047 | 1,853 | 615 | 604 | 569 | -- | 136 | 33,555 |
| **Hardwood species groups** | | | | | | | | | | | | | | | | |
| Eastern hardwood species groups | | | | | | | | | | | | | | | | |
| Select white oaks | 14 | 394 | 459 | 550 | 370 | 396 | 308 | 222 | 217 | 87 | 109 | 61 | -- | -- | -- | 3,190 |
| Hard maple | -- | -- | -- | -- | 8 | 13 | -- | -- | -- | -- | -- | -- | -- | -- | -- | 21 |
| Soft maple | -- | -- | 3 | 15 | 23 | 14 | 15 | -- | -- | -- | -- | -- | -- | -- | -- | 70 |
| Ash | 31 | 36 | 186 | 261 | 321 | 209 | 228 | 186 | 62 | 197 | 161 | -- | 84 | -- | -- | 1,960 |
| Cottonwood and aspen | 38 | 55 | 180 | 208 | 124 | 55 | 109 | 99 | 90 | 124 | 113 | -- | 139 | 82 | 379 | 1,794 |
| Basswood | -- | 7 | 5 | 2 | 4 | -- | -- | -- | -- | -- | -- | -- | -- | -- | -- | 17 |
| Other eastern soft hardwoods | 64 | 143 | 183 | 226 | 224 | 201 | 126 | 124 | 132 | 113 | 107 | 52 | -- | 142 | -- | 1,836 |
| Other eastern hard hardwoods | -- | -- | 5 | -- | 5 | -- | -- | -- | -- | -- | -- | -- | -- | -- | -- | 10 |
| Eastern noncommercial hardwoods | 98 | 87 | 44 | 16 | 10 | -- | -- | -- | -- | -- | -- | -- | -- | -- | -- | 254 |
| **All hardwoods** | 245 | 721 | 1,064 | 1,278 | 1,089 | 888 | 784 | 631 | 501 | 521 | 490 | 113 | 223 | 224 | 379 | 9,151 |
| **All species groups** | 491 | 1,339 | 2,581 | 5,426 | 6,871 | 6,338 | 5,782 | 4,603 | 3,549 | 2,374 | 1,105 | 717 | 792 | 224 | 515 | 42,706 |

All table cells without observations in the inventory sample are indicated by --. Table value of 0 indicates the aboveground tree biomass rounds to less than 1 thousand dry tons. Columns and rows may not add to their totals due to rounding.

57

Table 54.—Area of accessible forest land, in thousand acres, by Forest Survey Unit, county, and forest-land status, South Dakota, 2005

| Forest Survey Unit and county | Unreserved forests | | | Reserved forests | | | All forest land |
|---|---|---|---|---|---|---|---|
| | Timberland | Unproductive | Total | Productive | Unproductive | Total | |
| **Eastern** | | | | | | | |
| Belle Fourche-Grand-Moreau | 6 0 | 11 7 | 17 7 | - - | - - | - - | 17 7 |
| Cheyenne | 6 6 | - - | 6 6 | - - | - - | - - | 6 6 |
| White-Niobrara | 87 5 | 23 1 | 110 6 | - - | - - | - - | 110 6 |
| Bad-Missouri-Coteau-James | 102 5 | 19 4 | 121 8 | - - | - - | - - | 121 8 |
| Minnesota-Big Sioux-Coteau | 44 6 | 4 3 | 49 0 | - - | - - | - - | 49 0 |
| **Total** | 247 1 | 58 6 | 305 7 | - - | - - | - - | 305 7 |
| **Western** | | | | | | | |
| Belle Fourche-Grand-Moreau | 372 6 | 7 5 | 380 0 | - - | - - | - - | 380 0 |
| Cheyenne | 863 4 | 21 6 | 885 0 | 53 2 | - - | 53 2 | 938 1 |
| White-Niobrara | 58 2 | - - | 58 2 | - - | - - | - - | 58 2 |
| **Total** | 1 294 2 | 29 1 | 1 323 3 | 53 2 | - - | 53 2 | 1 376 4 |
| **All counties** | 1 541 3 | 87 6 | 1 629 0 | 53 2 | - - | 53 2 | 1 682 1 |

All table cells without observations in the inventory sample are indicated by -- Table value of 0 0 indicates the acres round to less than 0 1 thousand acres Columns and rows may not add to their totals due to rounding

Bad-Missouri-Coteau-James = Aurora Beadle Bon Homme Brown Brule Buffalo Campbell Charles Mix Davison Douglas Edmunds Faulk Gregory Hand Hanson Hughes Hutchinson Hyde Jerauld Jones Lyman McPherson Miner Potter Sanborn Spink Stanley Sully Walworth and Yankton counties

Belle Fourche-Grand-Moreau = Butte Corson Dewey Harding Lawrence and Perkins counties

Cheyenne = Custer Fall River Haakon Meade Pennington and Ziebach counties

Minnesota-Big-sioux-Coteau = Brookings Clark Clay Codington Day Deuel Grant Hamlin Kingsbury Lake Lincoln McCook Marshall Minnehaha Moody Roberts Turner and Union counties

White-Niobrara = Bennett Jackson Mellette Shannon Todd and Tripp counties

Table 55.—Area of accessible forest land, in thousand acres, by Forest Survey Unit, county, ownership group and forest-land status, South Dakota, 2005

| Forest Survey Unit and county | Forest Service | | Other Federal | | State and local government | | Undifferentiated private | | All forest land |
|---|---|---|---|---|---|---|---|---|---|
| | Timber-land | Other forest land | Timber-land | Other forest land | Timber-land | Other forest land | Timber-land | Other forest land | |
| **Eastern** | | | | | | | | | |
| Belle Fourche-Grand-Moreau | - - | - - | - - | 4 5 | - - | - - | 6 0 | 7 3 | 17 7 |
| Cheyenne | - - | - - | - - | - - | - - | - - | 6 6 | - - | 6 6 |
| White-Niobrara | - - | - - | 23 5 | 5 6 | - - | - - | 63 9 | 17 5 | 110 6 |
| Bad-Missouri-Coteau-James | - - | - - | 10 9 | - - | - - | - - | 91 6 | 19 4 | 121 8 |
| Minnesota-Big Sioux-Coteau | - - | - - | - - | - - | 4 3 | - - | 40 3 | 4 3 | 49 0 |
| **Total** | - - | - - | 34 4 | 10 1 | 4 3 | - - | 208 4 | 48 5 | 305 7 |
| **Western** | | | | | | | | | |
| Belle Fourche-Grand-Moreau | 293 6 | - - | 18 3 | - - | - - | - - | 60 7 | 7 5 | 380 0 |
| Cheyenne | 690 5 | 48 7 | 16 3 | 17 7 | 40 0 | 7 7 | 116 6 | 0 7 | 938 1 |
| White-Niobrara | - - | - - | 8 8 | - - | - - | - - | 49 4 | - - | 58 2 |
| **Total** | 984 0 | 48 7 | 43 5 | 17 7 | 40 0 | 7 7 | 226 7 | 8 1 | 1 376 4 |
| **All counties** | 984 0 | 48 7 | 77 8 | 27 8 | 44 3 | 7 7 | 435 2 | 56 7 | 1 682 1 |

All table cells without observations in the inventory sample are indicated by -- Table value of 0 0 indicates the acres round to less than 0 1 thousand acres Columns and rows may not add to their totals due to rounding

Bad-Missouri-Coteau-James = Aurora Beadle Bon Homme Brown Brule Buffalo Campbell Charles Mix Davison Douglas Edmunds Faulk Gregory Hand Hanson Hughes Hutchinson Hyde Jerauld Jones Lyman McPherson Miner Potter Sanborn Spink Stanley Sully Walworth and Yankton counties

Belle Fourche-Grand-Moreau = Butte Corson Dewey Harding Lawrence and Perkins counties

Cheyenne = Custer Fall River Haakon Meade Pennington and Ziebach counties

Minnesota-Big-sioux-Coteau = Brookings Clark Clay Codington Day Deuel Grant Hamlin Kingsbury Lake Lincoln McCook Marshall Minnehaha Moody Roberts Turner and Union counties

White-Niobrara = Bennett Jackson Mellette Shannon Todd and Tripp counties

Table 56.—Area of forest land, in thousand acres, by Forest Survey Unit, county/county group, and forest-type group, South Dakota, 2005

| County group | Spruce-fir | Other eastern softwoods | Pinyon-juniper | Ponderosa pine | Oak-hickory | Elm-ash-cottonwood | Maple-beech-birch | Aspen-birch | Other hardwoods | Exotic hardwoods | Nonstocked | All groups |
|---|---|---|---|---|---|---|---|---|---|---|---|---|
| Bad-Missouri-Coteau-James | - | 22 4 | - | - | 39 0 | 43 1 | - | - | - | 10 8 | 6 6 | 121 8 |
| Belle Fourche-Grand-Moreau | 24 2 | - | - | 313 7 | 28 3 | 6 0 | 3 0 | 12 4 | - | - | 10 2 | 397 7 |
| Cheyenne | 31 8 | - | 35 6 | 737 9 | 4 5 | 7 3 | - | 39 7 | 7 6 | - | 80 3 | 944 7 |
| Minnesota-Big Sioux-Coteau | - | - | - | - | 28 2 | 17 8 | - | - | - | - | 3 0 | 49 0 |
| White-Niobrara | - | 5 6 | - | 85 9 | 32 1 | 35 2 | - | - | 5 9 | - | 4 2 | 168 8 |
| Grand total | 56 0 | 28 0 | 35 6 | 1 137 5 | 131 9 | 109 3 | 3 0 | 52 0 | 13 6 | 10 8 | 104 3 | 1 682 1 |

All table cells without observations in the inventory sample are indicated by -- Table value of 0 0 indicates the acres round to less than 0 1 thousand acres  Columns and rows may not add to their totals due to rounding
Bad-Missouri-Coteau-James = Aurora  Beadle  Bon Homme  Brown  Brule  Buffalo  Campbell  Charles Mix  Davison  Douglas  Edmunds  Faulk  Gregory  Hand  Hanson  Hughes  Hutchinson  Hyde  Jerauld  Jones  Lyman  McPherson  Miner  Potter  Sanborn  Spink  Stanley  Sully  Walworth  and Yankton counties
Belle Fourche-Grand-Moreau = Butte  Corson  Dewey  Harding  Lawrence  Perkins counties
Cheyenne = Custer  Fall River  Haakon  Meade  Pennington and Ziebach counties
Minnesota-Big-Sioux-Coteau = Brookings  Clark  Clay  Codington  Day  Deuel  Grant  Hamlin  Kingsbury  Lake  Lincoln  McCook  Marshall  Minnehaha  Moody  Roberts  Turner and Union counties
White-Niobrara = Bennett  Jackson  Mellette  Shannon  Todd  and Tripp counties

Table 57.—Area of timberland, in thousand acres, by Forest Survey Unit, county, and stand-size class, South Dakota, 2005

| Forest Survey Unit and county | Stand-size class | | | | | All size classes |
|---|---|---|---|---|---|---|
| | Large diameter | Medium diameter | Small diameter | Chaparral | Nonstocked | |
| **Eastern** | | | | | | |
| Belle Fourche-Grand-Moreau | 6 0 | - - | - - | - - | - - | 6 0 |
| Cheyenne | 6 6 | - - | - - | - - | - - | 6 6 |
| White-Niobrara | 68 2 | 11 5 | 3 5 | - - | 4 2 | 87 5 |
| Bad-Missouri-Coteau-James | 40 8 | 39 1 | 16 0 | - - | 6 6 | 102 5 |
| Minnesota-Big Sioux-Coteau | 26 5 | 8 7 | 6 5 | - - | 3 0 | 44 6 |
| Total | 148 1 | 59 3 | 25 9 | - - | 13 8 | 247 1 |
| **Western** | | | | | | |
| Belle Fourche-Grand-Moreau | 257 5 | 56 2 | 58 9 | - - | - - | 372 6 |
| Cheyenne | 563 2 | 128 6 | 91 3 | - - | 80 3 | 863 4 |
| White-Niobrara | 44 5 | 2 3 | 11 5 | - - | - - | 58 2 |
| Total | 865 2 | 187 1 | 161 6 | - - | 80 3 | 1 294 2 |
| All counties | 1 013 3 | 246 4 | 187 6 | - - | 94 1 | 1 541 3 |

All table cells without observations in the inventory sample are indicated by -- Table value of 0 0 indicates the acres round to less than 0 1 thousand acres Columns and rows may not add to their totals due to rounding
Bad-Missouri-Coteau-James = Aurora Beadle Bon Homme Brown Brule Buffalo Campbell Charles Mix Davison Douglas Edmunds Faulk Gregory Hand Hanson Hughes Hutchinson Hyde Jerauld Jones Lyman McPherson Miner Potter Sanborn Spink Stanley Sully Walworth and Yankton counties
Belle Fourche-Grand-Moreau = Butte Corson Dewey Harding Lawrence and Perkins counties
Cheyenne = Custer Fall River Haakon Meade Pennington and Ziebach counties
Minnesota-Big-sioux-Coteau = Brookings Clark Clay Codington Day Deuel Grant Hamlin Kingsbury Lake Lincoln McCook Marshall Minnehaha Moody Roberts Turner and Union counties
White-Niobrara = Bennett Jackson Mellette Shannon Todd and Tripp counties

Table 58.—Area of timberland, in thousand acres, by Forest Survey Unit, county, and stocking class, South Dakota, 2005

| Forest Survey Unit and county | Stocking class of growing-stock trees | | | | | All classes |
|---|---|---|---|---|---|---|
| | Nonstocked | Poorly stocked | Moderately stocked | Fully stocked | Over-stocked | |
| **Eastern** | | | | | | |
| Belle Fourche-Grand-Moreau | - - | - - | - - | 6.0 | - - | 6.0 |
| Cheyenne | - - | - - | 6.6 | - - | - - | 6.6 |
| White-Niobrara | 4.2 | 54.8 | 28.5 | - - | - - | 87.5 |
| Bad-Missouri-Coteau-James | 16.5 | 51.7 | 18.4 | 15.9 | - - | 102.5 |
| Minnesota-Big Sioux-Coteau | 10.0 | 12.5 | 16.3 | 4.3 | 1.5 | 44.6 |
| Total | 30.7 | 119.0 | 69.8 | 26.2 | 1.5 | 247.1 |
| **Western** | | | | | | |
| Belle Fourche-Grand-Moreau | 7.5 | 103.8 | 219.9 | 41.4 | - - | 372.6 |
| Cheyenne | 96.6 | 439.3 | 265.7 | 61.7 | - - | 863.4 |
| White-Niobrara | 5.9 | 45.9 | 5.6 | 0.8 | - - | 58.2 |
| Total | 110.1 | 589.1 | 491.1 | 103.9 | - - | 1 294.2 |
| All counties | 140.8 | 708.1 | 560.9 | 130.1 | 1.5 | 1 541.3 |

All table cells without observations in the inventory sample are indicated by -- Table value of 0 0 indicates the acres round to less than 0 1 thousand acres  Columns and rows may not add to their totals due to rounding

Bad-Missouri-Coteau-James = Aurora  Beadle  Bon Homme  Brown  Brule  Buffalo  Campbell  Charles Mix  Davison  Douglas  Edmunds  Faulk  Gregory  Hand  Hanson  Hughes  Hutchinson  Hyde  Jerauld  Jones  Lyman  McPherson  Miner  Potter  Sanborn  Spink  Stanley  Sully  Walworth  and Yankton counties

Belle Fourche-Grand-Moreau = Butte  Corson  Dewey  Harding  Lawrence  and Perkins counties

Cheyenne = Custer  Fall River  Haakon  Meade  Pennington  and Ziebach counties

Minnesota-Big-sioux-Coteau = Brookings  Clark  Clay  Codington  Day  Deuel  Grant  Hamlin  Kingsbury  Lake  Lincoln  McCook  Marshall  Minnehaha  Moody  Roberts  Turner  and Union counties

White-Niobrara = Bennett  Jackson  Mellette  Shannon  Todd  and Tripp counties

62

Table 59.—Net volume of growing-stock and sawtimber (International 1/4-inch rule) on timberland by Forest Survey Unit, county, and major species group. South Dakota, 2005

| Forest Survey Unit and county | Growing stock | | | | | Sawtimber | | | | |
| | Major species group | | | | | Major species group | | | | |
| | Pine | Other softwoods | Soft hardwoods | Hard hardwoods | All species | Pine | Other softwoods | Soft hardwoods | Hard hardwoods | All species |
| | (in million cubic feet) | | | | | (in million board feet)[1] | | | | |
| **Eastern** | | | | | | | | | | |
| Belle Fourche-Grand-Moreau | -- | -- | 18.4 | -- | 18.4 | -- | -- | 83.8 | -- | 83.8 |
| Cheyenne | -- | -- | 8.0 | -- | 8.0 | -- | -- | 31.6 | -- | 31.6 |
| White-Niobrara | 37.2 | 2.8 | 10.0 | 18.3 | 68.2 | 160.1 | 11.5 | 33.6 | 64.7 | 270.0 |
| Bad-Missouri-Coteau-James | -- | 3.6 | 33.8 | 29.7 | 67.1 | -- | 13.5 | 119.2 | 63.0 | 195.7 |
| Minnesota-Big Sioux-Coteau | -- | 0.1 | 23.4 | 21.2 | 44.7 | -- | -- | 100.6 | 55.2 | 155.8 |
| Total | 37.2 | 6.5 | 93.5 | 69.2 | 206.4 | 160.1 | 25.0 | 368.8 | 182.8 | 736.8 |
| **Western** | | | | | | | | | | |
| Belle Fourche-Grand-Moreau | 535.9 | 39.5 | 14.0 | 10.9 | 600.4 | 2061.1 | 134.8 | 7.4 | 7.8 | 2211.2 |
| Cheyenne | 994.7 | 43.6 | 9.4 | 6.0 | 1053.7 | 3319.5 | 149.2 | 2.1 | 20.5 | 3491.3 |
| White-Niobrara | 35.0 | 0.9 | 0.5 | 1.4 | 37.7 | 138.9 | 2.3 | -- | -- | 141.2 |
| Total | 1565.6 | 84.0 | 24.0 | 18.2 | 1691.8 | 5519.4 | 286.3 | 9.6 | 28.3 | 5843.6 |
| All counties | 1602.8 | 90.5 | 117.5 | 87.4 | 1898.2 | 5679.6 | 311.4 | 378.3 | 211.1 | 6580.4 |

All table cells without observations in the inventory sample are indicated by — Table value of 0.0 indicates the volume rounds to less than 0.1 million cubic or board feet. Columns and rows may not add to their totals due to rounding

[1] International 1/4-inch rule

Bad-Missouri-Coteau-James = Aurora Beadle Bon Homme Brown Brule Buffalo Campbell Charles Mix Davison Douglas Edmunds Faulk Gregory Hand Hanson Hughes Hutchinson Hyde Jerauld Jones Lyman McPherson Miner Potter Sanborn Spink Stanley Sully Walworth and Yankton counties
Belle Fourche-Grand-Moreau = Butte Corson Dewey Harding Lawrence and Perkins counties
Cheyenne = Custer Fall River Haakon Meade Pennington and Ziebach counties
Minnesota-Big-sioux-Coteau = Brookings Clark Clay Codington Day Deuel Grant Hamlin Kingsbury Lake Lincoln McCook Marshall Minnehaha Moody Roberts Turner and Union counties
White-Niobrara = Bennett Jackson Mellette Shannon Todd and Tripp counties

Table 59a.—Net volume of growing-stock and sawtimber (Doyle rule) on timberland by Forest Survey Unit, county, and major species group, South Dakota, 2005

| Forest Survey Unit and county | Growing stock | | | | | Sawtimber | | | | |
|---|---|---|---|---|---|---|---|---|---|---|
| | Major species group | | | | | Major species group | | | | |
| | Pine | Other softwoods | Soft hardwoods | Hard hardwoods | All species | Pine | Other softwoods | Soft hardwoods | Hard hardwoods | All species |
| | (in million cubic feet) | | | | | (in million board feet)[1] | | | | |
| **Eastern** | | | | | | | | | | |
| Belle Fourche-Grand-Moreau | -- | -- | 18.4 | -- | 18.4 | -- | -- | 85.2 | -- | 85.2 |
| Cheyenne | -- | -- | 8.0 | -- | 8.0 | -- | -- | 19.8 | -- | 19.8 |
| White-Niobrara | 37.2 | 2.8 | 10.0 | 18.3 | 68.2 | 134.8 | 4.9 | 21.1 | 41.4 | 202.2 |
| Bad-Missouri-Coteau-James | -- | 3.6 | 33.8 | 29.7 | 67.1 | -- | 6.1 | 111.2 | 35.6 | 152.9 |
| Minnesota-Big Sioux-Coteau | -- | 0.1 | 23.4 | 21.2 | 44.7 | -- | -- | 74.1 | 35.1 | 109.2 |
| Total | 37.2 | 6.5 | 93.5 | 69.2 | 206.4 | 134.8 | 11.0 | 311.4 | 112.1 | 569.3 |
| **Western** | | | | | | | | | | |
| Belle Fourche-Grand-Moreau | 535.9 | 39.5 | 14.0 | 10.9 | 600.4 | 1 331.5 | 79.0 | 3.4 | 3.5 | 1 417.4 |
| Cheyenne | 994.7 | 43.6 | 9.4 | 6.0 | 1 053.7 | 2 059.5 | 85.1 | 0.9 | 11.8 | 2 157.2 |
| White-Niobrara | 35.0 | 0.9 | 0.5 | 1.4 | 37.7 | 99.8 | 0.8 | -- | -- | 100.6 |
| Total | 1 565.6 | 84.0 | 24.0 | 18.2 | 1 691.8 | 3 490.7 | 164.9 | 4.3 | 15.3 | 3 675.2 |
| All counties | 1 602.8 | 90.5 | 117.5 | 87.4 | 1 898.2 | 3 625.5 | 175.9 | 315.7 | 127.4 | 4 244.5 |

All table cells without observations in the inventory sample are indicated by -- Table value of 0 0 indicates the volume rounds to less than 0 1 million cubic or board feet Columns and rows may not add to their totals due to rounding
[1] Doyle rule

Bad-Missouri-Coteau-James = Aurora Beadle Bon Homme Brown Brule Buffalo Campbell Charles Mix Davison Douglas Edmunds Faulk Gregory Hand Hanson Hughes Hutchinson Hyde Jerauld Jones Lyman McPherson Miner Potter Sanborn Spink Stanley Sully Walworth and Yankton counties
Belle Fourche-Grand-Moreau = Butte Corson Dewey Harding Lawrence and Perkins counties
Cheyenne = Custer Fall River Haakon Meade Pennington and Ziebach counties
Minnesota-Big-sioux-Coteau = Brookings Clark Clay Codington Day Deuel Grant Hamlin Kingsbury Lake Lincoln McCook Marshall Minnehaha Moody Roberts Turner and Union counties
White-Niobrara = Bennett Jackson Mellette Shannon Todd and Tripp counties

Table 65.—Sampling errors by Forest Survey Unit and county for area of timberland, volume, average annual net growth, average annual removals, and average annual mortality on timberland, South Dakota, 2005

| Forest Survey Unit/County group | Area of forestland (acres) | Sampling error | Area of timberland (acres) | Sampling error | Growing-stock volume on timberland (cubic feet) | Sampling error | Sawtimber volume on timberland (board feet) | Sampling error |
|---|---|---|---|---|---|---|---|---|
| 1 Bad-Missour -Coteau-James | 121,844 | 17.22 | 102,467 | 19.32 | 67,107,702 | 28.98 | 195,657,029 | 37.82 |
| 1 Be e Fourche-Grand-Moreau | 17,687 | 51.63 | 5,962 | 100.24 | 18,403,612 | 100.24 | 83,760,026 | 100.24 |
| 1 Cheyenne | 6,621 | 96.16 | 6,621 | 96.16 | 7,990,032 | 96.16 | 31,606,750 | 96.16 |
| 1 M nnesota-B g S oux-Coteau | 48,959 | 29.84 | 44,616 | 31.13 | 44,657,559 | 41.92 | 155,784,667 | 54 |
| 1 Wh te-N obrara | 110,602 | 20.46 | 87,473 | 23.92 | 68,239,288 | 27.81 | 269,958,695 | 28.97 |
| 2 Be e Fourche-Grand-Moreau | 380,045 | 10.52 | 372,580 | 10.61 | 600,373,067 | 12.49 | 2,211,158,947 | 13.68 |
| 2 Cheyenne | 938,120 | 4.98 | 863,352 | 5.43 | 1,053,718,290 | 8.05 | 3,491,299,018 | 10.04 |
| 2 Wh te-N obrara | 58,247 | 29.56 | 58,247 | 29.56 | 37,726,743 | 33.34 | 141,160,726 | 34.74 |
| All county groups | 1,682,125 | 3.33 | 1,541,319 | 3.62 | 1,898,216,293 | 5.21 | 6,580,385,857 | 6.58 |

Th s report ut zes a samp ng error based on one standard error wh ch means the chances are two n three that had a 100-percent nventor taken us ng these methods, the resu ts wou d have been w th n the m ts nd cated.

County groups:

Bad-M ssour -Coteau-James = Aurora, Bead e, Bon Homme, Brown, Bru e, Buffa o, Campbe , Char es M x, Dav son, Doug as, Edmunds, Fau k, Gregory, Hand, Hanson, Hughes, Hutch nson, Hyde, Jerau d, Jones, Lyman, McPherson, M ner, Potter, Sanborn, Sp nk, Stan ey, Su y, Wa worth, and Yankton count es

Be e Fourche-Grand-Moreau = Butte, Corson, Dewey, Hard ng, Lawrence, and Perk ns count es

Cheyenne = Custer, Fa R ver, Haakon, Meade, Penn ngton, and Z ebach count es

M nnesota-B g-s oux-Coteau = Brook ngs, C ark, C ay, Cod ngton, Day, Deue , Grant, Ham n, K ngsbury, Lake, L nco n, McCook, Marsha , M nnehaha, Moody, Roberts, Turner, and Un on count es

Wh te-N obrara = Bennett, Jackson, Me ette, Shannon, Todd, and Tr pp count es

Note: Cheyenne and Wh te N obara county groups span forest survey un t boundar es